The Complete Halogen Oven Cookbook

Other books by Sarah Flower:

 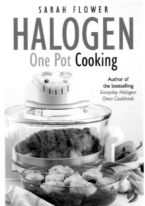

For advice about cooking with your halogen oven
visit www.everydayhalogen.com

Write or phone for a catalogue to:

How To Books
Spring Hill House, Spring Hill Road, Begbroke, Oxford OX5 1RX
Tel: 01865 375794

Or email: info@howtobooks.co.uk

Visit our website www.howtobooks.co.uk to find out more about us and our books.

Like our Facebook page **How To Books & Spring Hill**
Follow us on **Twitter @Howtobooksltd**

Read our books online www.howto.co.uk

The Complete Halogen Oven Cookbook

How to cook Easy and Delicious Meals
using your Halogen Oven

SARAH FLOWER

SPRING HILL

Published by Spring Hill, an imprint of How To Books Ltd.
Spring Hill House, Spring Hill Road
Begbroke, Oxford OX5 1RX
United Kingdom
Tel: (01865) 375794
Fax: (01865) 379162
info@howtobooks.co.uk
www.howtobooks.co.uk

First published 2013

How To Books greatly reduce the carbon footprint of their books by sourcing their
typesetting and printing in the UK.

British Library Cataloguing in Publication Data
A catalogue record of this book is available from the British Library.

ISBN: 978 1 908974 03 7

Produced for How To Books by Deer Park Productions, Tavistock, Devon
Designed and typeset by Mousemat Design Ltd
Printed and bound by in Great Britain by Bell & Bain Ltd, Glasgow

NOTE: The material contained in this book is set out in good faith for general guidance
and no liability can be accepted for loss or expense incurred as a result of relying in
particular circumstances on statements made in the book. Laws and regulations are
complex and liable to change, and readers should check the current position with relevant
authorities before making personal arrangements.

Contents

Introduction

It has been really lovely to hear about readers' experiences when using their halogen. The success of my first book about cooking with a halogen oven, *The Everyday Halogen Oven Cookbook*, has shown that this amazing gadget really has taken off. Families, single people, elderly people, students, those who stay in holiday homes and even caravanners all love the benefits the halogen can offer. I use mine every day and would be lost without it. I am really pleased we can now offer you this new book, fully illustrated in wonderful colour. We have taken the best recipes from the entire halogen series of books, as well as adding in lots of new ones to help inspire you. I do hope you like it as much as I do.

As ever, I love hearing from you, so visit the halogen website at www.everydayhalogen.com for tips, reviews and more recipes for your halogen oven, or my own site at www.sarahflower.co.uk. You can also follow my tweets at #Mssarahflower.

Enjoy the book!

Sarah xx

Chapter 1
How to use your halogen oven

Just as I did in my first halogen book, I've written this first introductory chapter to show any newbie halogen users how to get the most from your machine. If you have bought my other books, you may want to skip this chapter as it will contain duplicate information.

Choosing the right machine for you

There are many different halogen ovens on the market, but they are basically all the same machine. My first machine was from JML, when halogen ovens first started to become popular. I was not really sure what to expect and over time, the oven has gained more and more use in our home. The two main variations are in the size of the bowl and whether the lid is on a hinge or not. Personally, I would opt for the largest bowl as this increases the usability of the oven. You can also purchase height extension rings which can help maximize use. Since using the JML, I progressed to use the Flavorwave Turbo Platinum Oven. Out of all the machines I have used, this is one of the best – it has a hinged lid, digital settings, a 3-speed fan and a preheat setting. Lakeland also do a great halogen oven with a hinged lid. It also had a rotating arm, similar to the actifry, which is great when cooking wedges or chips but it also help transfer the hot air under the racks, claiming this makes for a more thorough cooking.

Looking at online forums I have noticed that lids are a bit of a bugbear amongst users. I had a lid stand beside my JML machine, though annoyingly these are optional extras you have to purchase and are quite flimsy to look at. In my opinion, if you can afford to buy the halogen cooker with the hinge lid, it is definitely a safer and easier option.

How do they work?

The halogen oven/cooker is basically a large glass bowl with an electric halogen lid. The lid is heavy as it contains the halogen element, timer and temperature settings. It can be fiddly to clean but I will come to that later. The halogen bulbs heat up the bowl and the fan moves the air around the bowl to create an even temperature. As it is smaller than a conventional oven, it heats up faster, reducing the need for long preheating and in some cases, reduces the overall cooking time. This makes it a very popular choice for those watching their pennies, living on their own or like me, living with a busy family. It has even become a popular choice for students and caravanners. I read on a forum that some caravanners use the self-clean facility just like a mini dishwasher – ingenious! It is also popular as a second oven and really becomes invaluable at busy times like Christmas.

For safety, the handle of the lid has to be in place (placed securely down) for the machine to turn on. This means that when you lift the lid, it automatically cuts off the machine. If you are using a machine with the hinged lid, you have to press the start button to start and remember to turn the machine off when you lift the lid.

A halogen oven does cook slightly differently to a conventional oven, so there is often a period of trial and error when you first start, but in fact the differences are not vast. If you have favourite recipes that you cook in the conventional oven, try them in the halogen. I find cooking at a slightly lower temperature or cooking for less time normally gives the same results, but hopefully this book will help give you more confidence.

The halogen oven is not a microwave and does not work in the same way as a microwave, so if you are thinking you can cook food in minutes you are wrong. It does, however, have a multitude of skills – defrosting, baking, grilling, roasting and steaming are all perfect for the halogen oven. Remember that to get the optimum benefit, air needs to circulate around the bowl, so ideally place the food on racks and avoid the temptation to over fill.

Using your oven

Getting the right equipment

This sounds obvious but... make sure you have oven trays, baking sheets and casserole dishes that will fit inside the halogen oven – there is nothing more frustrating than planning a meal and then realising just at the last minute that it does not fit in the machine! You can use any ovenproof dish or trays – metal, silicon and Pyrex are all fine. The halogen oven is round so it makes sense to look at trays and stands of the same shape, just smaller so you can remove them without burning yourself! This is probably the only real issue I have with the oven. When I first started using a halogen oven, it was frustrating to find that 80% of my bakeware did not fit in the machine. A quick rethink and purchase of the relevant accessories have proved invaluable. If money is tight, remember that you don't have to spend a fortune on new cookware – you will often find great casserole dishes at boot sales or charity shops.

You can buy an accessories pack, which contains steamer pans, grilling pans, toasting racks and even a height extension ring. These packs are highly recommended if you use your oven regularly and will certainly enhance what you can do with the machine. There are many places on the web selling these, so a general search will point you in the right direction. Amazon is also a great place to look.

Let there be light

As experienced halogen users will know, the halogen light will turn on and off during cooking. This is not a fault of the thermostat, as some people have mentioned on forums. The light is designed to turn off when the programmed temperature is reached, and then turn on again when the temperature drops. Set your required temperature and marvel at how quickly the oven reaches it – literally in minutes. I love the light – there is something quite cosy about walking into your kitchen on a winter or autumn evening to see the glow of the halogen cooker, along with the ability to watch your food cook.

Timings

Halogen ovens come with a timer (up to 60 minutes) and temperature setting dials. The Flavorware Turbo also comes with 3 fan settings and digital timer. All halogens turn off when the timer settings have been reached. This means you can be reassured that if the phone rings or you are called away from the kitchen, your food won't spoil.

Size

The oven is small enough to sit on a worktop, but do allow space for removal of the lid if this is not hinged. The lid can get very hot and is quite large and heavy, being the brains of the machine, so it is often a good idea to buy the lid stand. Do be careful when using this, though, as the stand is quite flimsy to look at until you get used to it. You could opt to place the lid on a heatproof surface – again, be careful not to burn yourself or your worktop! As with all electrical and hot appliances, do not let your children near it – the glass bowl gets very hot.

Carefully does it

Your oven should come with a tong-type gadget to help you lift out the racks. The tongs supplied with the over are usually are quite useful, but I also use a more substantial set of tongs. As with any oven or cooker, do be careful as the bowl and contents get very hot. I find using proper oven gloves a necessity as they cover all of your hand and wrist and can prevent accidents.

Foil and coverings

Some people like to use foil when cooking. It can be a good idea to use foil to prevent something browning too quickly or to parcel foods; however, if you do this, make sure your parcels are secure. The fan is very strong and if the foil is not secure it can float around the oven and could damage the element. Another option to prevent burning is obviously to turn the temperature down or place the food further away from the element (on the low rack, or add a height extension ring).

Cleaning your oven

Your oven is promoted as being self cleaning – this basically means that you just need to fill it with a little water, add a squirt of washing up liquid and turn it on to the wash setting. The combination of the fan and the heat allows the water to swish around the bowl giving it a quick clean. This normally takes about 10 minutes. Personally I find it just as simple to remove the bowl and place it in the dishwasher – it always comes out gleaming. The lid is a little more difficult to clean and for this I would refer to the manufacturer's guidelines as each product can be a little different. Do not get the element or electrical parts wet!

High and low racks

There are two standard racks which come with every halogen oven: a low rack, and a high rack (not to be confused with the rack I use for grilling!). The high rack is nearer the element, so use this more if you want to brown something. The low rack is used more for longer cooking times. You can also cook directly on the bottom of the bowl. I have done this quite often, particularly if I am being lazy and just chucking in some oven chips or doing a bit of roasting. It does cook well but will take a little longer as compared to using the racks, as air is not able to circulate all around the food.

Grilling

If you want to grill something you really need to get the rack as high as possible. The two racks you get with the halogen oven (low and high) may not be suitable for quick grilling, though if these are all you have it will work, but just take longer. I have purchased an accessory pack and in this you get a toasting rack (with egg holes). This can be used as a grilling rack, either on its own or with a baking tray on top. As the food is nearer the element, grilling times are much quicker – you can grill cheese on toast in approximately 3-4 minutes.

Baking

Some people worry about using the oven to make cakes. Things can go a bit wrong if you set the oven temperature too high – resulting in a cake with a crusty brown top and a soggy middle. Setting the oven to a lower temperature can solve this problem. Muffins and cupcakes take between 12 and 18 minutes. You only really get a problem with cakes if you are cooking for too long at too high a temperature. Try some of my cake recipes and you will see how simple it can be.

To preheat or not to preheat…

Most recipes I have found on forums don't mention preheating. This is probably due to the speed the oven reaches its required temperature; however, I think it is often worth turning the oven on 5 minutes before use just to bring it up to the right temperature. I found this to be the case when attempting to cook soft boiled eggs. According to the Flavorware recipe book I should be able to cook a soft egg in 6 minutes just by placing it on the high rack. It did not work… However, I tried again having preheated the oven and it was much more successful. Because the halogen only takes a few minutes to reach its set temperature, I believe it is best to preheat, therefore most of my recipes advise this. Some machines have a preheat button (such as the Flavorware, which preheats at 260°C for 6 minutes), but others (such as the JML) require you to set to the required temperature and turn on.

I hope this chapter has not confused you. Move on to try some recipes and then come back to this chapter at a later date – it will probably make more sense then!

Enjoy!

Liquids

Metric	Imperial	US cups
5ml	1 tsp	1 tsp
15ml	1 tbsp	1 tbsp
50ml	2fl oz	3 tbsp
60ml	2½ fl oz	¼ cup
75ml	3fl oz	⅓ cup
100ml	4fl oz	scant ½ cup
125ml	4½ fl oz	½ cup
150ml	5fl oz	⅔ cup
200ml	7fl oz	scant 1 cup
250ml	10fl oz	1 cup
300ml	½ pt	1¼ cups
350ml	12fl oz	1⅓ cups
400ml	¾ pt	1½ cups
500ml	20fl oz	2 cups
600ml	1pt	2½ cups

Weight

Metric	Imperial
25g	1oz
50g	2oz
75g	3oz
100g	4oz
150g	5oz
175g	6oz
200g	7oz
225g	8oz
250g	9oz
300g	10oz
350g	12oz
400g	14oz
450g	1lb

Measurements

Metric	Imperial
5cm	2in
10cm	4in
13cm	5in
15cm	6in
18cm	7in
20cm	8in
25cm	10in
30cm	12in

Oven temperatures

Metric	Imperial
110°C	225°F
120°C	250°F
140°C	275°F
150°C	300°F
160°C	325°F
180°C	350°F
190°C	375°F
200°C	400°F
220°C	425°F
230°C	450°F
240°C	475°F

Chapter 2
Snacks

Halogen ovens aren't just for main meals or desserts – they are perfect for quick and easy snacks. I included quite a comprehensive list of snacks in The Everyday Halogen Oven Cookbook, including the basics such as toast, bacon, garlic bread and frozen chips, but here are some other suggestions, along with some simple tips you can adapt to suit. Unlike microwaves, halogen ovens can heat up pastries, pizzas and snacks without resulting in a soggy mess. They can also make delicious toasties, warmed bagels, bruschetta – and you can even use them to boil an egg! Don't forget you can also steam, bake, roast or grill vegetables, and here are some great suggestions to help enhance your cooking experience.

Crumpets

There is nothing like the taste of hot buttered crumpets. You could add some crumbled Stilton for a savoury variation – yummy!

1. To prepare, preheat your halogen oven using the preheat setting or turn the temperature to the highest setting as you are ready to grill.

2. Place the crumpets on the high rack and grill until your reach your desired level of toastedness.

3. If you are adding a topping, add this after the crumpets have started to brown and not at the beginning of the whole process.

4. Serve hot.

Quesadillas

These are savoury filled tortillas – I make them up like a giant sandwich and then cut it into wedges before serving. Feel free to fill yours with any savoury ingredients you like. This recipe is for a basic cheese, tomato, onion and chilli quesadilla.

1. Place one floured tortilla on your greased baking tray.

2. Sprinkle with your chosen fillings. Season to taste.

3. Place the remaining tortilla on the top and press down firmly.

4. Place on the high rack. Set the temperature to 210°C and cook for 5–8 minutes until the tortilla is golden and the filling starts to melt.

5. Cut into wedges and serve with salsa and guacamole dips.

Ingredients:

2 tortillas

1 onion, sliced

1–2 tomatoes, sliced

½ chilli, finely sliced

30g mature Cheddar, grated

Seasoning to taste

17

Pesto Bagel Pizza

1–2 bagels

1–2 tbsp pesto

1–2 tomatoes, sliced

30g grated mature
    Cheddar

This is my favourite bagel combination. Perfect with a lovely sesame or seeded bagel.

1. Place the bagels on the grill rack (see grilling section in Chapter 1, How to use your halogen oven). Turn the temperature to 250°C and cook for 2–3 minutes.

2. Remove from the oven and spread with pesto. Add the slices of tomato and finish with the grated cheese. Season to taste.

3. Place back on the grill rack and cook for another couple of minutes until the cheese starts to melt and bubble.

4. Serve immediately whilst still warm.

Bacon

Who can resist a bacon butty? You can cook your bacon, without adding more fat, in approximately 6 minutes using the halogen oven.

1. Place your bacon on the high or grill rack.

2. Set the temperature to 240°C.

3. Cook for 5 minutes, then turn over and cook for another 5 minutes, or until you reach your desired level of crispiness.

Chapter 3

Meat

The halogen oven can cook meat slightly quicker than the conventional oven, though you have to be careful to get your temperature settings right. If you have the temperature too high, the tops of the joints or bird will burn whilst the middle may remain raw or undercooked. I would advise using a temperature gauge to test your meat, particularly poultry or joints of meat, until you are more confident – even when following a recipe.

When meat is placed on the lower rack, the juices and fats will drain away, therefore making the meat healthier. Some people worry that the meat will dry out too much with this method of cooking, but to be honest, meat does tend to be very tender and moist when cooked in the halogen oven – unless you overcook it! If you are concerned, you can always place your meat on a baking tray instead of the rack, or even cook it on the base of the bowl – which is ideal if you also want to add roast potatoes.

If you are cooking a joint you can cook as you would do in a conventional oven – roughly 20 minutes per 500g at 180°C, and add then another 10 minutes at the end of the cooking time.

As with all foods cooked in the halogen oven, make sure there is adequate space between the element and the food – ideally at least 2–3cm. The nearer the food is to the element, the more likely it is to burn or cook quickly. If you are concerned, wrap some foil over the food for the first half of the cooking time, though do make sure you secured it well, as the power of the fan could lift the foil off.

Roast Leg of Lamb with Roasted Vegetables

Ingredients:

1 leg of lamb

3–4 cloves of garlic, crushed

½ tsp chopped chillies

Rosemary sprigs

Seasoning

2–3 tbsp olive oil

2 onions

2–3 carrots

2 sweet potatoes

6–8 potatoes

2–3 tsp paprika

2–3 tsp semolina

2–3 tsp olive oil

There is no reason why you can't cook a roast in your halogen oven – roast potatoes are especially brilliant cooked this way. Obviously, much depends on the size of your halogen oven so do check this before you buy your leg of lamb!

1. Preheat your halogen oven using the preheat settings, or turn on to 210°C.

2. Mix together the garlic, chilli and olive oil to form a paste. Rub this over the leg of lamb. You can score the flesh first to help give the paste something to hold on to. Pierce the skin and push in some rosemary sprigs. Sprinkle over a little salt and black pepper, to your own taste.

3. Place on the lower rack and cook for 15 minutes. Meanwhile cut the potatoes into your preferred size and steam or parboil for 10 minutes. Drain and place the potatoes back in the empty saucepan. Add the paprika and semolina. Pop the lid back on the saucepan and shake to fluff up and coat the potatoes.

4. Place the potatoes around the lamb, and brush them with olive oil. Halve the onions, cut your carrots into chunks, and place them with the potatoes. Remember to turn the lamb and vegetables regularly and add a brush of oil or paste as required.

5. Cook for another 10 minutes before turning down to 180°C and cooking for another 30–45 minutes or until both the meat and potatoes are cooked to your satisfaction. Timings for lamb depend on the size of the joint.

Pepperoni, Olive and Red Onion Pizza

Serves
2–4

To save time, you could make your own dough in advance. Roll it out and place each piece on greased foil or a parchment sheet. Stack the pizza bases on top of each other, cover in cling film or foil and refrigerate until ready to use.

1. Sift the flour into a bowl. Mix the water, yeast, sugar and oil together. Make sure the sugar is dissolved. Make a well in the middle of the flour and pour in.

2. Mix thoroughly before transferring the dough onto a floured board. Knead well until the dough springs back when pulled.

3. Place the dough in a floured bowl and cover with cling film or a warm, damp cloth until it has doubled in size. This takes about 1 hour.

4. Knead again, and divide into 4 pieces. This dough can be stored in the fridge or freezer until needed.

5. When you're ready to prepare your pizza, roll the dough out to the desired thickness and size. Cover with a small layer of tomato pasta sauce or tomato purée. Sprinkle with cheese before adding the pepperoni, red onion rings and olives. Season to taste.

6. I normally place my pizza on a sheet of greased tinfoil and cook directly on the lower rack. You can buy tins with holes in which allow the base of pizzas or pies to brown.

7. Turn your halogen oven to 200°C and cook for 10–15 minutes until golden.

8. Due to the force of the fan, if you have loose toppings you may want to place the high rack face down on top of the pizza. I would suggest you spray it with a little oil first, to prevent sticking. You only need to do this for the first half of the cooking time.

Ingredients:

For the dough
500g strong bread flour
325ml warm water
1 sachet of dried yeast
1 tsp brown sugar
2 tbsp olive oil

For the topping
2–3 tbsp tomato pasta
   sauce or tomato purée
50–75g grated mature
   cheese
1 red onion, cut into rings
8–10 slices of pepperoni
8–10 olives

Coq au Vin

Olive oil

10–12 shallots whole, or
   small red onions,
   quartered

2 cloves of garlic, crushed

1 pack of lean bacon or
   lardons, chopped

250g button mushrooms

2 carrots, diced

2 sticks of celery, finely
   sliced

400g chicken breast or
   thigh pieces

1 tin of chopped tomatoes

200ml red wine

1 bay leaf

Handful of chopped
   parsley

2–3 sprigs of fresh thyme

Seasoning to taste

This is another family favourite in the Flower home. I like to serve this with either roast potatoes or roasted mini new potatoes and tenderstem broccoli.

1. Preheat your halogen oven using the preheat setting or set the temperature to 210°C.

2. In an ovenproof casserole dish, add the oil, onion and garlic. Place in the halogen oven and cook until the onion starts to soften.

3. Add the mushrooms, carrots, celery and chicken pieces and cook for another five minutes before adding all the remaining ingredients. Combine well and season to taste.

4. Cover with a lid or double-wrapped tin foil, securely fastened.

5. Place back on the low rack and cook for 40–50 minutes until the vegetables and chicken are cooked to taste.

6. Serve with buttered potatoes garnished with parsley, and green vegetables, or a green salad.

Chicken Burgers

Serves

4

It's not just the kids who like burgers, so why not make your own healthier versions? These are really tasty and can be frozen until needed. Serve with wholemeal or granary baps for a healthier treat.

1. Place all the ingredients in a food processor and mix thoroughly.

2. When mixed, form into balls – these should be firm but moist. If the mixture is dry, add some beaten egg.

3. Use the palm of your hand to flatten the balls into burger shapes.

4. You can place them the fridge until you are ready to use them, or freeze them in layers (separate each layer with parchment to prevent them sticking together).

5. When you are ready to cook the burgers, brush lightly with olive oil. Turn the halogen oven to 250°C. Place on the high rack and cook for them for 4–5 minutes on each side until golden. (You are actually grilling them at this heat!)

6. Serve with white or wholemeal baps, a salad garnish and a dollop of mayonnaise.

Ingredients:

1 onion, chopped

1–2 cloves garlic, crushed

1 stick of celery, chopped

½ red pepper, chopped

500g chicken mince

30g pine nuts

Small handful of freshly chopped parsley

1 tbsp home-prepared wholemeal breadcrumbs

Ingredients:

3 tbsp maple syrup or
    honey
1 tbsp mustard
1 tbsp Worcestershire
    sauce
1 tbsp soy sauce
2 tsp paprika
4 chicken drumsticks

Sticky Chicken Drumsticks

These really are sticky but very, very tasty!

1. Place all the ingredients apart from the chicken in a bowl and mix well.

2. Meanwhile, score the drumsticks with a sharp knife to give the marinade something to hold on to.

3. Have a large freezer bag ready – this can get messy! Place the drumsticks and the marinade in the large freezer bag. Shake well to ensure they are thoroughly coated. Secure and leave in the fridge overnight.

4. When you are ready to cook, as a precaution, line your halogen oven with foil to collect any mess. Turn on to 230°C.

5. Place the drumsticks on the high rack. You can place them directly onto the rack or, if you prefer, you can have them on a baking tray.

6. Cook the chicken gently on both sides, adding marinade as you go if you prefer. The advantage of cooking straight on the rack that the oven will cook the meat on all sides.

7. You will still need to turn it over, however, to get an even browning. Make sure that your chicken is thoroughly cooked – this should take about 15–20 minutes depending on the size of the drumsticks.

8. Serve with couscous and salad.

Roast Beef with Horseradish

Serves
4–6

A great family roast – serve it with roast potatoes, Yorkshire puddings, steamed vegetables and home-made gravy. Timings will vary depending on the size of the joint and your own personal taste. If you like a pinker beef, test a little earlier.

1. Preheat your halogen oven using the preheat setting or set the temperature to 210°C.

2. In a mixing bowl, combine the sugar, golden syrup and horseradish. Season well with black pepper.

3. Place the beef joint on a roasting tin and place on the low rack. Cook for 20 minutes before turning the temperature down to 180°C.

4. Coat well with the sticky horseradish sauce and cook for a further 20 minutes for every 450g. If it starts to darken too much whilst cooking, you can cover securely with tin foil.

5. Halfway through cooking add the red wine – this will mix with the beef juices and can be used for your beef gravy stock.

6. Once your beef is cooked, wrap in tin foil and leave to rest for at least 20 minutes. Use this time to make your gravy using the natural juices in the roasting pan. Mix 1 tsp cornflour with a little stock and add it to the roasting pan. Heat gently and stir well as it thickens, to avoid any lumps. Serve with roast potatoes, Yorkshire puddings and steamed vegetables.

Ingredients:

Beef joint

2 tbsp golden syrup

2 tbsp dark brown sugar

4 tbsp horseradish

Black pepper

300ml red wine

Cheat's Leftover Chicken Pie

Serves

4–6

This is my mum's recipe. Now my brother Mark and I have grown up and flown the nest, mum and dad have had to adapt to cooking for two instead of four. This meal is made from the leftovers of mum's Sunday roast, so they usually tuck into it early in the week.

1. Heat the oil and fry the onion in a pan, add the celery, mushrooms, cooked chicken, and ham if using, and cook for 3–4 minutes.

2. Add the soup and heat for a further 3 minutes.

3. Place the mixture in an ovenproof pie dish, making sure it fits in the halogen oven. Roll out your pastry larger than required. Wet the edges of the dish with milk or water, and cut thin strips of pastry to place on the edge of the pie dish – dampen again with milk. This will give the top pastry something to hold on to. Cut the top pastry to size and place over the pie. Crimp and seal the edges thoroughly.

4. Place on the low rack, set the temperature to 200°C and cook for 20–30 minutes until the pie crust is golden.

Ingredients:

A drizzle or spray of olive
  oil
1 onion, chopped
2 sticks of celery, chopped
75g mushrooms, quartered
200–300g cooked chicken
  (removed from bone)
100g cooked ham
  (optional)
1 can condensed chicken
  or mushroom soup
Half a pack of ready-made
  puff pastry

Beef Lasagne

For the bolognese sauce

1 onion finely chopped

2–3 cloves garlic, finely
  chopped

A spray of olive oil

1 pepper, finely chopped
  (optional)

400g lean beef mince or,
  for vegetarians, veggie
  mince

150ml red wine

75g mushrooms, finely
  chopped (optional)

3–4 fresh tomatoes,
  chopped, or 1 tin
  chopped tomatoes

Mixed herbs to taste

Seasoning to taste

For the white sauce

25g butter

1 tbsp plain flour or
  cornflour

500–750ml milk

¼ tsp mustard (optional)

Black pepper to taste

Sheets of lasagne (ensure
  the pack says 'no
  precooking required')

Grated cheese to garnish

I normally make up a large batch of bolognese sauce and use this to make lasagne, spaghetti bolognese and chilli. You can freeze this so why not prepare two and freeze one uncooked?

1. Fry the onion and garlic in a little olive oil until soft and translucent. Add the pepper if using one.

2. Add the mince and cook until brown, followed by the wine and mushrooms if using them, and cook for 2 more minutes.

3. Add the tinned or fresh tomatoes (or 'cheat' pasta sauce), stirring well. Finally, add the herbs and season to taste. Leave to simmer for 5 minutes.

4. While the bolognese mix is simmering, make the white sauce. Melt the butter gently in a saucepan on a medium heat (not high!). Add the flour or cornflour and stir well with a wooden spoon. Add the milk, a little at a time, continuing to stir to avoid lumps.

5. Switch now to a balloon whisk. Continue to stir over a medium heat until the sauce begins to thicken. The balloon whisk will also help eradicate any lumps that may have formed. Add more milk as necessary to get the desired thickness. The sauce should be the thickness of custard. Add the mustard and season with black pepper.

6. Preheat your halogen oven using the preheat setting, or set the temperature to 200°C.

7. Spoon a layer of bolognese mix into the bottom of your lasagne dish (make sure this fits into your halogen oven), and then pour over a thin layer of white sauce, followed by a layer of lasagne sheets. Continue alternating the layers, finishing with the white sauce. Don't overfill the dish as the lasagne may spill out during cooking.

8. Sprinkle grated cheese over the sauce.

9. Place on the low rack in the halogen oven and cook at 200°C for 40–50 minutes, until the top is golden and the lasagne sheets are cooked. If the top starts to get too dark, cover it with tin foil, making sure it is secure. (The cooking time can be greatly reduced if you use fresh lasagne sheets.)

10. Serve with salad and garlic bread.

Shepherd's and Cottage Pie

Serves
4–6

The difference between shepherd's pie and cottage pie is the meat. Shepherd's pie traditionally is made with lamb mince and cottage pie with beef. Nowadays you can make these dishes using a variety of minced meat or vegetarian mince if you prefer.

1. Place the potatoes and the 2 chopped carrots in a steamer and cook until soft.

2. Meanwhile, heat the oil in a large sauté pan and fry the onion for 1–2 minutes before adding the mince.

3. Cook until brown before adding the 2 cubed carrots, the mushrooms and the wine.

4. Dissolve the yeast extract in the hot stock before adding to the mince. Cook for 15 minutes until the mince is tender and reduced to the desired consistency. Season to taste and add a dash of Worcestershire sauce.

5. Mash the steamed potato and carrots together. Add the butter and two thirds of the Cheddar. Mix thoroughly.

6. Place the mince in a deep ovenproof dish and spoon the mash over the top. Be careful not to overfill the dish. Press the mash down gently with a fork. Top with the remaining grated cheese and a sprinkle of paprika.

7. Set the temperature to 200°C. Place on the low rack and cook in the oven for 20–25 minutes.

Ingredients:

- 800g potatoes, cut into rough chunks
- 4 carrots, 2 roughly chopped, 2 cut into small cubes
- A spray of olive oil
- 1 onion, chopped
- 400g lean mince (or pre-drained of fat)
- 75g mushrooms, sliced (optional)
- 100ml red wine
- 1 tsp yeast extract (Marmite or similar)
- 200ml meat stock, or vegetable stock if using veggie mince
- Seasoning to taste
- Worcestershire sauce
- 25g butter
- 75g mature Cheddar
- Paprika for sprinkling

Arrabiata Chicken Bake

Chilli oil

1 onion, sliced

2 red peppers, sliced

1 red chilli, finely sliced

2–3 cloves of garlic,
  roughly chopped

3–4 chicken fillets, diced

1 jar of pasta sauce
  (ideally chilli and
  tomato)

1 tin of chopped tomatoes

1 pack wholemeal tortillas

300g crème fraîche

200ml milk

75g mature Cheddar

Black pepper

4–6 cherry tomatoes,
  halved

This can be prepared in advance and left until you are ready to cook.

1. Add the oil to your sauté pan, and place on a medium heat. Add the onion, peppers, chilli, garlic and chicken and cook until the chicken starts to turn white all over.

2. Add the pasta sauce and chopped tomatoes and cook for another 10 minutes.

3. While that is cooking, mix the milk, crème fraîche and cheese together. Season with black pepper.

4. Divide the chicken mixture between the tortillas and roll – this can be messy! Place the rolled up tortillas in an ovenproof dish. Pour the crème fraîche mixture over the tortillas. Finish with a few of the tomato halves.

5. Place the dish in the halogen oven on the low rack.

6. Set the temperature to 180°C and cook for 20 minutes until golden and bubbling. Serve immediately.

Roasted Herby Vegetables and Chicken Legs

A wholesome one pot dish with a delicious flavour – I really love the tomatoes when they are roasted and sweet. You can prepare the chicken legs beforehand and place in the fridge, but bring them up to room temperature before cooking. Serve with a nutritious green salad.

1. In a large bowl, add the potatoes, peppers and onion. Add paprika and olive oil and combine until well coated.

2. Pour this into an ovenproof dish (or place directly in the halogen). Set the temperature to 200°C. Add more oil if necessary. Cook for 15 minutes.

3. Finely chop your herbs (you can use a mini electric chopper for this). Add the crushed garlic and 1–2 tablespoons of olive oil. Combine well.

4. Rub half of this mixture over your chicken drumsticks. Add these to your potatoes and cook for another 15 minutes before adding the tomatoes. Drizzle remaining herbs over the whole dish and combine well. Add more oil if necessary. Turn the drumsticks throughout cooking to get an even cook.

5. Bake for another 20–30 minutes until the vegetables and chicken are cooked.

Ingredients:

Olive oil
600g small new potatoes, washed
2 tsp paprika
1 red onion, quartered
Large handful of fresh mixed herbs (such as thyme, rosemary, oregano)
3–4 cloves of garlic, crushed
4–6 chicken legs
1–2 red peppers, thickly sliced
12–15 small vine tomatoes, whole

Serves

4–6

Ingredients:

1 whole chicken

1 red onion

1 lemon

30g butter

1–2 tsp herbs

Roast Chicken

I have converted my dad into a halogen oven fan. He now likes cooking his chicken in the halogen oven as it creates a really juicy and succulent bird. Remember, the key is to cook it upside down for the first half of the cooking time as this allows the juices to run into the breast meat. You may have to juggle with the chicken and roasts if you have a small halogen oven.

1. Wash and prepare your chicken according to your own preference. I place a red onion or a lemon, both cut in half, in the cavity of the bird to enhance the flavour. I then rub the skin with butter and sprinkle with herbs. You can also place herb butter under the skin.

2. Place the chicken, breast side down, on the lower rack and turn the halogen oven to 240°C for 25 minutes.

3. Turn the chicken back over so the breast side is up, reduce the temperature to 210°C and cook for another 40 minutes until it is cooked through; the timings obviously depend on the size of the bird. As with all meats, make sure the meat is thoroughly cooked before eating.

4. The fat will have drained to the base of the halogen oven. You can use some of this juice to make your gravy.

5. Serve with stuffing balls, roast potatoes and seasonal vegetables.

Moussaka

Serves

4

I have a friend who is not keen on aubergines and so when she cooks this recipe she swaps the aubergine slices for thinly sliced potato. This dish can be frozen so why not prepare two and freeze one uncooked? It really does save you time and money.

1. Place the aubergines in a pan of boiling water for 2 minutes. Remove and pat dry. Leave to one side.

2. Meanwhile, heat a little olive oil in a sauté pan and fry the onion and garlic. Add the lamb mince and cook until brown.

3. Add the tomatoes, tomato purée, mint, cinnamon and seasoning and cook for another 2–3 minutes.

4. Select your ovenproof dish – I normally use a Pyrex lasagne dish for this. Make sure it fits into your halogen oven. Preheat your halogen oven – either select the preheat function, if applicable, or set to 210°C.

5. Place a layer of mince in an ovenproof dish, followed by a layer of aubergine. Continue alternating mince and aubergine, finishing with a layer of mince.

6. Mix the crème fraîche with the grated cheese and pour over the final layer of mince. Garnish with a sprinkle of Parmesan.

7. Place on the low rack in the halogen oven and cook for 20–25 minutes until bubbling.

Ingredients:

2–3 aubergines, sliced

1 onion

2 cloves garlic, crushed

Olive oil

400g lamb mince

1 tin chopped tomatoes

2 tsp tomato purée

1 tsp dried mint

2 tsp ground cinnamon

Seasoning to taste

300ml low fat crème fraîche

50g mature Cheddar or Parmesan cheese, grated

Tandoori Chicken

1 onion, finely chopped

2–3 cloves garlic, crushed

1 tsp ground coriander

1 tsp cayenne pepper

1 tsp chilli powder (or
    fresh chillies, finely
    chopped)

1 tbsp curry powder

2 tsp turmeric

2–3 tsp paprika

2.5cm (1in) knuckle of
    ginger, grated

Juice and zest of 1 lemon

3–4 tomatoes

1 tsp tomato purée

2 tbsp olive oil

200g low fat natural
    yoghurt

4 large pieces of chicken
    (or you can use any
    leftover chicken)

You can cheat with this recipe and use a shop-bought tandoori paste. However, I prefer to make this myself – there is something deeply satisfying about flinging around herbs and spices when cooking, and it is a great way to get the family's attention as the flavours start to waft around the house.

1. Place the onion, garlic, herbs and spices with the lemon juice, zest, tomatoes, tomato purée, olive oil and yoghurt in a food processor and whizz together. Place this in an ovenproof dish.

2. Add the chicken pieces and combine thoroughly. For the best flavour, leave the chicken to marinate for a few hours.

3. When you are ready, preheat your halogen oven using the preheat setting, or set the temperature to 200°C.

4. Place your ovenproof dish on the low rack and cook for 20–25 minutes.

5. Serve on a bed of rice.

Parma Wrapped Chilli Chicken

Serves
4

A very simple dish that takes minutes to prepare but packs a punch. Serve with new minted potatoes and green salad.

1. Preheat your halogen oven using the preheat setting, or set the temperature to 200°C.

2. Place the quark or cream cheese in a bowl and mix in the chilli and tabasco sauce until combined. Season to taste.

3. Using a sharp knife, cut slits in the chicken breasts to form a pocket. Stuff the pockets with the creamed mixture.

4. Wrap securely with Parma ham. Place, with the seam underneath, on a greased ovenproof dish. Drizzle with olive oil and season to taste.

5. Place on the low rack and cook for 20–30 minutes until the chicken is cooked.

6. Serve with a lovely salad.

Ingredients:

4 chicken breasts

3-4 tbsp quark or low fat cream cheese

1 red chilli, finely chopped

1 tsp chilli powder

Few drops of tabasco sauce (to taste – optional)

Seasoning to taste

8 slices of Parma ham (you can use bacon if you prefer)

Olive oil

Puffed Sausage Rolls

Ingredients:

Puff pastry

Sausage meat

Beaten egg to glaze

A sprinkle of sesame seeds
   (optional)

These are perfect for a packed lunch or picnic treat. You can make your own pastry using a standard shortcrust mix if you prefer this to puff pastry. I would use 200g plain or wholemeal flour and 100g of butter. Rub the butter into the flour until it resembles breadcrumbs, then gradually add cold water to form a dough. Refrigerate for 20 minutes before rolling out.

1. Roll your sausage meat into a thumb-thick length.

2. Roll out your pastry to the desired size and thickness (it should be just over twice as wide as your roll of sausage meat, and 1cm longer at each end).

3. Place the sausage mix 1–2cm from the long edge of the pastry.

4. Coat the edges of the pastry with beaten egg before folding it over the sausage meat. Press down firmly on the edge before cutting the sausage rolls to the desired length.

5. Preheat your halogen oven using the preheat settings or turn on to 210°C.

6. Place the sausage rolls on a baking tray. Brush them with beaten egg and sprinkle with sesame seeds before placing the tray on the low rack and baking in the oven for 25 minutes, until golden brown. You may need to turn these if the underside is not cooked thoroughly.

Variations

For a great variation to the standard sausage roll, mix some herbs with the sausage meat to create delicious Herby Sausage Rolls. If you like things hot, mix your sausage meat with some fresh chillies and a dollop of tabasco sauce to create tempting Hot, Hot, Hot Sausage Rolls. Vegetarians can opt for any of the above by mixing with vegetarian sausage mix.

Spicy Meatballs in Rich Tomato Sauce

Serves
4–6

It's a good idea to make the meatballs in advance. If you double up the recipe, you can place the surplus meatballs on a baking tray lined with greaseproof paper and just pop it in the freezer. Once frozen you can bag them – this way they don't get bashed and you can pull out the required number of meatballs as and when you need them!

    If you are making this recipe for children, reduce the chilli.

1. Combine all the meatball ingredients together in a bowl and mix thoroughly.

2. Form the mixture into small balls and place on a baking sheet. Cover the balls with a sheet of cling film and store in the fridge for 30 minutes to rest.

3. Preheat your halogen oven using the preheat setting, or turn the temperature to 200°C.

4. Place your meatballs in the bottom of an ovenproof dish, making sure it fits in your halogen oven. Drizzle with a little oil and place on the low rack for 15 minutes, rolling/turning halfway through.

5. While that is cooking combine the tomatoes, garlic, sugar, salt, drizzle of olive oil and chopped basil leaves.

6. Remove the meatballs from the oven and cover with the tomato mixture. Place back on the low heat for another 15 minutes before serving with some spaghetti.

Ingredients:

For the meatballs
400g beef mince
1 small onion, finely chopped or grated
1 tsp paprika
1 tsp cumin
1 chilli, finely chopped
1 tsp chilli powder
2 tsp Worcestershire sauce
1 tsp parsley
50g breadcrumbs
1 egg, beaten
Seasoning to taste
Drizzle of olive oil

For the tomato sauce
400g tin chopped tomatoes (or fresh tomatoes, chopped)
2 cloves garlic, crushed
1 tsp sugar
½ tsp salt
Handful of chopped basil leaves
Drizzle of olive oil

Traditional Cornish Pasties

Ingredients:

For the shortcrust pastry

150g plain flour

75g cold butter

5–6 tbsp cold water

For the pasty filling

1 onion

1 carrot

1 potato

100g swede

350g lean rump steak

1 tsp paprika

1 tsp mixed herbs
  (optional)

Seasoning to taste

As I live on the Cornish border, it seems appropriate to include a traditional Cornish staple. Pastry doesn't always cook well in the halogen – especially the bottoms of dishes. To avoid a soggy bottom, turn the pasties and cook them upside down until completely browned.

1. Make the pastry. Place the flour in a large bowl and add the chilled butter, cut into small pieces. Using your fingertips, rub the butter into the flour until the whole mix resembles breadcrumbs. Add 5–6 tablespoons of cold water (a little at a time) and mix until it forms a dough. Wrap the dough in cling film and place in the fridge to cool until needed.

2. Chop the vegetables and steak into small dice-sized pieces.

3. Place in a bowl and mix thoroughly. Add the paprika and herbs and season well.

4. Roll out the pastry on a floured surface until even. Using a small round plate approximately 20cm in diameter as a template, cut 4 circles.

5. Preheat your halogen oven using the preheat setting, or set the oven temperature to 210°C.

6. Place some of the steak and vegetable mix in the centre of each circle – do not overfill. Use beaten egg or water to brush the edges of the pastry before bringing the edges together and crimping until sealed.

7. Place the pasties on a lined baking tray. Brush with beaten egg.

8. Place on the high rack and bake in the oven for 20 minutes until the pastry starts to turn golden. Reduce the heat to 150°C,

move to lower rack and cook for a further 20 minutes. As the halogen is not always great at pastry, turn the pasties over so that the bottoms are facing upwards and cook for another 10–15 minutes.

9. Remove from the oven and place on a cooling rack or serve immediately.

Lamb Biryani

Olive oil

1 large onion, diced

2-3 cloves of garlic,
   crushed

500g lamb, cubed

1 tsp ground cinnamon

1 tsp ground cardamon

1 tsp ground cloves

1 tsp curry powder

250ml plain Greek yoghurt

4 tomatoes, diced

250g long grain rice

Toasted almonds, for
   sprinkling on top

You will be surprised how simple this dish really is. You can prepare this in advance.

1. In a sauté pan, add the oil and heat until hot. Add the lamb, onion and garlic and cook until the lamb starts to brown and the onion starts to soften.

2. Add the spices and cook for a couple of minutes before adding the yoghurt and tomatoes. Combine well and cook on a low heat gently.

3. Meanwhile cook your rice as directed by the manufacturer. I normally add 1½ cups of water to every 1 cup of rice, bring to the boil and leave simmering for a couple of minutes before popping a lid on and removing completely from heat. Leave to stand for 10–12 minutes. Fluff up using a fork.

4. When the rice is done, place a layer in the bottom of your ovenproof dish. Follow this with a layer of the lamb mixture. Continue until you have used up all the ingredients.

5. Cover with foil and place on the medium rack. Turn the temperature to 180°C and cook for 20 minutes.

6. Garnish with the toasted almonds before serving.

Moroccan Style Chicken and Vegetable Tagine

Serves

4

I love using spices to create new dishes – this recipe uses a lot of spices, but allow them to infuse and the taste is amazing. If you don't like things too hot you can omit the chilli.

1. Chop the chicken into chunks. Place in a bowl.

2. In a food processor add 2 tbsp of olive oil, the spices, chilli, ginger, half the chopped herbs and the tomatoes. Whizz to form a marinade.

3. Pour this onto the chicken and cover with clingfilm. Leave to marinate overnight or for at least 2 hours. When you are ready to cook, bring the chicken back up to room temperature for at least 1 hour.

4. Place a little olive oil in your sauté pan on a medium heat. Add the onion, garlic and pepper and cook for 3–5 minutes before adding the chicken, holding back most of the marinade until you add the remaining ingredients.

5. Cook for 5 minutes before adding pepper, potatoes, carrot, green beans and chickpeas, plus the stock and the marinade.

6. Simmer gently for 10 minutes before adding the remaining herbs and transfer into an ovenproof stock pot.

7. Pop on a lid or double layer of foil. Place on the low rack and cook at 180°C for 30–40 minutes.

8. Serve with couscous, scattered with a few toasted pine nuts.

Ingredients:

Olive oil
3–4 chicken fillets, diced
2.5cm knuckle of ginger, finely chopped
1 tsp paprika
1 tsp cumin
1 tsp turmeric
1 tsp cinnamon
Small handful of mint leaves
Small handful of coriander leaves
1 chilli, finely diced
1 tin of chopped tomatoes
1 large onion, sliced
2 cloves of garlic, roughly chopped
1 green pepper, thickly diced
2 sweet potatoes, peeled and cut into chunks
1 carrot, diced
60g green beans
1 tin of chickpeas, drained
300–400ml chicken stock

Chapter 4
Fish

We should all eat more oily fish. Packed with essential omega 3 fatty acids, oily fish should be included in at least three meals a week. Choose from mackerel, trout, salmon, sardines, pilchards, and herring. The halogen is great for cooking fish, whether grilled, baked, roasted or parcelled. Experiment with your favourite dishes.

Healthy Tip! Swapping your red meat for omega rich oily fish will not only reduce your risk of colorectal cancer but fish also has great anti-inflammatory properties. And the omega 3 essential fatty acids found in oil rich fish such as salmon are known to decrease the production of inflammatory proteins, which can help protect you from joint problems such as arthritis. It has also been shown to help protect you from Alzheimer's, and in children can increase concentration, memory and improve behaviour. We really should all eat more! If you don't like fish, I would strongly recommend taking a fish oil supplement (not cod liver oil). Make sure it is good quality.

Serves

4

Ingredients:

4 salmon fillets
1 lemon
Lemon juice
12 vine tomatoes
Olive oil
Sea salt
Black pepper
1 red onion, diced
1 ripe avocado, diced
1 red chilli, finely chopped
1 red pepper, diced
Zest and juice of a lime
Half a cucumber, diced
Small handful chopped
   mint leaves
Extra virgin olive oil
Seasoning to taste

Baked Salmon with Minted Salsa and Roasted Tomatoes

Salmon is packed with omega 3 fatty acids. Combined with the tomatoes and nutrient-rich salsa, this really is a very healthy meal.

1. Place each salmon fillet in the centre of a piece of foil. Add one or two slices of lemon on top of the salmon fillets. Finish with an extra squeeze of lemon juice and season to taste. Wrap and place on a baking tray.

2. Place the tomatoes on another baking tray, keeping their stalks intact. Drizzle with a little olive oil, sprinkle with sea salt and black pepper.

3. Place the salmon in the oven on the high rack. Set the temperature to 190°C and cook for 15–20 minutes or until cooked to your own personal taste.

4. Add the tomatoes on the low rack or base of the halogen 10–12 minutes before the salmon should be cooked.

5. Meanwhile place the salsa ingredients (all remaining ingredients apart from the olive oil) together in a bowl and mix well.

6. Drizzle with olive oil and a squeeze of lime.

7. Place the salmon on your plate with the baked tomatoes. Top with the salsa and finish with a drizzle of extra virgin olive oil and a few mint leaves. Serve with a lime wedge to the side.

Baked Salmon with New Potato Salad and Yoghurt Dressing

1. Place the fillets on a square of foil, drizzle with lemon juice, scatter with lemon zest and season with black pepper. Seal the parcel, place on a baking tray and leave until ready to cook.

2. Place in the oven on the low rack. Set the temperature to 200°C and cook for 15–20 minutes or until cooked to your own personal taste.

3. Meanwhile, steam your potatoes until just soft.

4. Remove from the steamer and add the spring onion and chives. Combine well, and season to taste.

5. In a bowl mix the yoghurt, lemon juice, parsley and seasoning.

6. Mix some of the yoghurt dressing with the potatoes, leaving some to pour onto the salmon

7. Place the potatoes on a plate, top with a few slices of cucumber, and then place the salmon on top of that. Drizzle with remaining yoghurt dressing.

8. Serve with a leafy salad.

Ingredients:

4 salmon fillets
Juice and zest of 1 lemon
Black pepper
1kg new potatoes, cut in half
Small bunch of spring onions, finely chopped
Small bunch of chives, finely chopped
150g fat free Greek yoghurt
1–2 tbsp lemon juice
Handful of chopped parsley
Black pepper to season
¼ cucumber, finely sliced

Creamy Fish Pie

1kg potatoes

500g fish fillets, or ask
your fishmonger for
pieces of flaky white fish

200g salmon pieces
(optional)

100g prawns or mussels
(optional)

2 leeks, sliced

250ml milk

25g butter

25g flour

1 tsp mustard

Seasoning to taste

A little grated cheese for
topping

This is another family favourite. You can make this as one large dish or a couple of smaller dishes. Why not use sweet potatoes to create a golden yet nutritious topping?

1. Boil or steam the potatoes until tender. Once cooked, mash with a little butter and place to one side.

2. Meanwhile place the fish and milk in a pan and bring the milk to the boil. Reduce the heat and cook gently for 10 minutes or until the fish is cooked through.

3. Drain the fish and reserve the liquid for making the sauce.

4. Flake the fish and place in your pie dish.

5. Steam the leeks and combine with the fish.

6. To make a creamy sauce, melt the butter in a pan and add the flour. Cook for a minute before stirring in the reserved milk stock.

7. Heat gently, stirring continuously, until the sauce thickens. I normally use a whisk at this stage as it helps prevent any lumps from forming. Add the mustard and season to taste.

8. Pour the sauce over the fish.

9. Preheat your halogen oven using the preheat setting, or set the temperature to 200°C.

10. Cover the fish with mashed potato and top with a small amount of grated cheese.

11. Place in the halogen oven on the low rack. Bake for 20–25 minutes until golden on top.

Salmon, Sweet Potato and Chilli Fish Cakes

Serves
4

This is a healthy way to make fish cakes, which are traditionally deep fried (and not so healthy!). This recipe uses the halogen oven to bake or grill the fish cakes. Serve them with a delicious homemade salsa, new potatoes and salad.

1. Mix the fish, cooked and mashed sweet potato, spring onions, chillies, cumin, lemon juice and herbs together in a bowl. Add a little beaten egg to bind if needed. Season to taste.

2. Form the mixture into cakes. If your mixture is a bit too wet, add a little plain flour. Place on greased baking parchment and chill in the fridge for 10 minutes.

3. Preheat the halogen oven using the preheat setting, or set the temperature to 250°C.

4. Remove your fish cakes from the fridge, and brush them with a light coating of olive oil.

5. Place the fish cakes directly on the high rack, or you can use either a baking tray or browning pan.

6. Cook the cakes for 5–6 minutes each side, turning halfway through to ensure they are evenly cooked and browned. (You are actually grilling them at this heat!)

7. Serve with a lovely salad and chilli dip.

Ingredients:

- 300g cooked or tinned salmon
- 350g sweet potatoes, cooked and mashed
- 3–4 spring onions, finely chopped, including green stalks
- 2 chillies, finely chopped
- 1 tsp ground cumin
- 1 tbsp lemon juice
- Small handful of coriander leaves, finely chopped
- 1 egg, beaten

Simple Baked Trout

Ingredients:

4 whole trout

1–2 tbsp butter

Small handful of fresh
   herbs, finely chopped

1 lemon, sliced

1–2 dsp water

Olive oil

Black pepper

Trout is packed with protein and omega 3 essential fatty acids. This recipe is easy to follow, but feel free to add whatever herbs you wish – I use a combination of parsley, thyme and chives.

1. Mix the butter and herbs together in a bowl to form a herb butter.

2. Place your trout on buttered foil almost double the size of the trout. Drizzle lemon juice over the trout.

3. Where the trout has been filleted, stuff with a herb butter and a slice or two of lemon. Add 1–2 dessertspoons of water. Drizzle with a dash of olive oil and season with black pepper.

4. Set temperature to 200°C.

5. Seal the foil securely and place on a baking tray or directly on the low rack. Cook for 20–30 minutes until the fish is tender and flaking.

6. Serve with new potatoes and green vegetables.

Serves

4

Ingredients:

4 mackerel, cleaned,
    gutted, with heads and
    tails removed

Olive oil

Black pepper

2–3 tbsp horseradish

Juice and zest of 1 lemon

1 onion, finely chopped

Small handful of fresh
    thyme, finely chopped

Small handful of fresh
    parsley, finely chopped

Grilled Mackerel

Mackerel is another great source of omega 3 essential fatty acids and it is also high in protein.

1. Score the fish on each side and brush with olive oil. Sprinkle with black pepper.

2. Place on the grill rack (see Chapter 1, How to use your halogen). You are going to grill the mackerel so set the temperature to maximum. Grill for approximately 6 minutes each side.

3. While the mackerel is grilling, mix the remaining ingredients together. Season to taste. If you want a creamier sauce you can add a tablespoon or two of cream or crème fraîche.

4. Place a spoonful of the sauce over the mackerel. Serve with new potatoes and salad.

Red Snapper and Tomato Bake

Serves

4

Red snapper is packed with protein, selenium, vitamin D and phosphorus.

1. Place your fish fillets in an ovenproof dish. Season to taste.

2. In a sauté pan, add the oil, garlic and red onion. Fry until starting to become translucent.

3. Add the tomatoes, wine and half the basil to the sauté pan. Cook for another 2–3 minutes. Remove and pour over the fish.

4. Cover the ovenproof dish with foil. Bake on the low rack for 20 minutes at 190°C, until the fish is cooked.

Ingredients:

500g red snapper fillets
Olive oil
2 cloves of garlic, crushed
1 red onion, finely
    chopped
50g sundried tomatoes,
    chopped
3 ripe vine tomatoes
200ml red wine
Handful of chopped fresh
    basil

Herb Stuffed Sea Bass

Serves

2

Sea bass has a mellow flavour but is packed with omega 3 essential fatty acids, protein and vitamins A and D.

1. Wash the fish and leave to one side.

2. Chop the herbs and place in a bowl. Add the lemon zest and juice, breadcrumbs, and tomato and combine. Season to taste.

3. Place the olive oil in a sauté pan and gently cook the onion and lardons. Drain, retaining the oil from the pan. Place the onion and lardons with the herb mixture and combine well.

4. Stuff the fish with the herb mixture. For added decoration you can add some sprigs of herbs so they flare out of the fish.

5. Score the top of the fish with a sharp knife. Brush generously with the oil from the sauté pan.

6. Place the fish in your ovenproof dish. Put the dish on the low rack. Set the temperature to 170°C and cook for 20–30 minutes until cooked to your taste. Cooking times may vary depending on the size of the fish. If the fish starts to get too dark, cover securely with foil.

7. Serve with lemon wedges, salad and new potatoes.

Ingredients:

2 sea bass, gutted and cleaned (you can remove the head if you prefer)
Small handful of fresh parsley, finely chopped
Small handful of fresh dill, roughly chopped
Small handful of fresh thyme, roughly chopped
Juice and zest of half a lemon
3 tbsp wholemeal breadcrumbs
1 large tomato, finely chopped
50ml white wine
Olive oil
1 red onion, finely chopped
150g lardons

Baked Pesto Fish

Ingredients:

4 fish fillets (opt for coley,
    cod or pollack)

3–4 tbsp pesto

Olive oil

Black pepper

I have chosen coley for this dish, but you can choose any similar fish fillet, such as cod or pollack. Speak to your fishmonger for more suggestions.

1. Place each fillet in a square of baking parchment or foil, large enough to secure around the fish.

2. Cover fillet with a thick layer of pesto. Drizzle with a dash of olive oil and season with black pepper.

3. Seal the parcels and place on a baking tray.

4. Place in the oven on the high rack and set the temperature to 200°C. Cook for 15–20 minutes until fish is tender and flaking.

5. Serve with new potatoes and green vegetables.

Salmon Kebabs

Serves
4

These are also great on barbecues. Remember, if you are using wooden skewers, you will need to soak them overnight before you use them – otherwise they will just catch fire on your barbecue!

1. If you are using wooden skewers, you will need to soak them overnight!

2. Cut the salmon into chunks and place in a bowl.

3. Mix the honey, soya sauce, ginger, lemon zest and olive oil together. Season to taste. Mix this with the salmon. Leave to marinate for 1 hour.

4. When you are ready to cook, thread the potato, courgette, salmon and peppers onto your skewers.

5. Brush or spray with a little olive oil and season to taste.

6. Place on a baking tray on the grill rack. Set the temperature to high and grill, turning occasionally for 10–12 minutes until thoroughly cooked.

7. Drizzle with any remaining marinade. Serve with some savoury rice.

Ingredients:

- 1 large salmon fillet
- 2–3 tbsp runny honey
- Soya sauce (dash or to taste)
- 2cm knuckle of ginger, finely grated
- Zest of ½ lemon
- 1 tbsp olive oil
- Seasoning to taste
- 350g new potatoes, cooked
- 2 courgettes, cut into thick chunks
- 1 red pepper, cut into thick chunks
- 1 yellow pepper, cut into thick chunks

Grilled Sardines with Mustard Dressing

6 tomatoes, finely
  chopped
1–2 cloves of garlic
Olive oil
8–12 sardines (allow 2-3
  per person depending
  on size)
2 tbsp olive oil
1 tbsp wholegrain mustard
Black pepper and sea salt
  to taste
1 tsp sugar
Zest of 1 lemon
Crusty bread

A posh version of sardines on toast!

1. Chop the tomatoes and stir in the garlic. Drizzle with a little olive oil. Season with black pepper, sea salt and a light sprinkle of sugar. Combine well.

2. Place on a baking tray and place on the high rack and cook for 10 minutes at 210°C.

3. Meanwhile, wash the fish, remove the heads and slit from head to tail. Open out the fish and lay it skin side up. Press along the back bone with the heel of your hand. Flip it over and carefully remove all the bones. Season to taste with black pepper.

4. Remove the tomatoes and leave to one side.

5. Place on the grill rack. You are going to grill at the highest temperature for 3–4 minutes each side. Times depend on the size of the fish. For the last few minutes of cooking, place the tomato mixture on the low rack (to heat through) or if you prefer, heat gently in a pan.

6. Meanwhile mix the oil, mustard, sugar and lemon zest together. Season to taste.

7. Place a large slice of crusty or French bread on the plates. Place the tomato mixture over the bread and finish with the sardines. Drizzle with the mustard dressing and season to taste. Add some fresh herbs to garnish.

Ingredients:

125g spinach

1 small onion

225g cream cheese

1 egg

Black pepper

Pinch of nutmeg

75g peas (thaw first if
    using frozen peas)

400g uncooked salmon,
    cut into 2.5cm chunks

80g uncooked French
    beans, cut into 2.5cm
    lengths

200g crème fraîche

Juice of half a lemon

2 tbsp milk

Small handful of freshly
    chopped dill

Salmon and Spinach Terrine

This is a really impressive and tasty dish. It is vital, however, to chill it overnight in order for it to set. I am quite generous with my black pepper when I make this recipe, but you can taste as you add your pepper to create the right seasoning for you. You can use low fat cream cheese for this recipe, as a healthier option, although you may find the terrine is a little wetter if you keep it for more than a day.

1. Place the spinach in a food processor. Add the onion and egg and season very generously with black pepper. Whizz until roughly combined. Don't over blend.

2. Remove from the processor and stir in the cream cheese and peas.

3. Grease a 1lb loaf tin well. If you are concerned about removing the terrine from the tin when it's done, you could use a liner suitable for loaf tins.

4. Place a layer of the spinach mixture in the bottom of the tin. Place a layer of salmon over this, followed by a layer of the French beans (you can lay the beans in rows to make a nice pattern when cutting the terrine).

5. Add another layer of the spinach mixture, followed by the salmon and finish with the remaining spinach. Press down firmly.

6. Cover with foil, making sure it is secure.

7. Place an ovenproof deep-sided dish on the low rack. Make sure your loaf tin fits inside this. Fill the ovenproof dish with hot water, until it reaches just over halfway up the outside of the loaf tin (it's easier to do this once the tin is on the rack as it avoids the risk of burning yourself!).

8. Turn the temperature to 180°C and cook for 25 minutes.

9. Remove from the oven and leave to cool completely.

10. Once cool place in the fridge overnight.

11. To make the sauce, mix the crème fraîche, lemon, milk and dill together and season to taste.

Cod Romanesco

You can of course use any white fish fillet for this. I normally prepare the romanesco-style topping in advance.

1. Place all the ingredients apart from the cod and half the parsley in a food processor and whizz until roughly combined.

2. Place a thick layer of the mixture over each of the fillets.

3. Place in a greased ovenproof dish and pop this on the low rack.

4. Set the temperature to 190°C and cook for 20 minutes, or until the fish flakes easily (timing depends on size of the fillets).

5. Serve with new potatoes and French beans.

Ingredients:

1–2 chillies, depending on taste

3 cloves of garlic

6–8 sundried tomatoes (the ones soaked in oil), drained

½ tsp paprika

40g of cashew nuts

2 tbsp of olive oil (or can use oil from sundried tomatoes)

Small handful fresh parsley

4 plump cod fillets

Chapter 5
Vegetarian

Vegetarian food is not just for vegetarians. There are some delicious meals that will satisfy most meat eaters as well as vegetarians. If you like the texture of meat but want to reduce saturated fat from your diet, why not opt for quorn? Quorn mince can be used as a direct swap for meat mince recipes. You can also buy a wide range of Quorn products. Experiment more with beans and pulses. They increase the level of protein in your diet (which can help keep you fuller for longer and slows down the absorption of carbohydrates) but also packed with fibre to help keep your bowels healthy.

Vegetables are packed with antioxidants, vitamins and phytonutrients. Steam or stir-fry rather than boil. To maintain a healthy diet you should ideally eat two or three oily fish meals per week, no more than two meat dishes and two or three vegetarian meals per week. Try not to rely too heavily on cheese in your meals. If you are a cheese addict, opt for mature cheeses (as you need to use less to create flavour) and low fat versions.

Vegetable and Butterbean Cobbler

This is a very filling meal, so you really don't need to serve it with anything else.

1. Heat a little olive oil in an ovenproof casserole dish on your hob. (Remember to make sure the dish will fit comfortably in your halogen oven as it will need to be transferred at a later stage). Add all the vegetables (not the tomatoes or butterbeans) and cook for 5 minutes.

2. Add tomatoes and sundried tomato paste, and cook for further 5 minutes – stirring well to avoid sticking.

3. Add the paprika, chopped parsley, vegetable stock and butterbeans. Bring up to the boil and cook for 10 minutes.

4. Remove from the hob, cover and place on the low rack of the halogen oven. Cover with a lid or double layer of foil, making sure this is secure. Set the temperature to 190°C and cook for 30 minutes.

5. Meanwhile, place the flour in a bowl, and add the yoghurt, oil and chopped parsley. Mix together to make a soft dough. Place on floured board and shape into individual balls. Flatten slightly.

6. When your vegetable stew has cooked, remove the lid or foil and stir the casserole. Add more vegetable stock if needed. Place the scones on the top of the casserole, forming a circle or completely covering the top of the casserole. You should be able to do this without having to lift out the casserole, but be careful not to burn yourself.

7. Continue to bake for another 20 minutes (until the scones are golden and fluffy).

8. Serve immediately.

Ingredients:

For the vegetable stew
Olive oil
2 red onions, cut into wedges
2 cloves of garlic, crushed
1 leek, sliced
1 large carrot, diced
2 sticks of celery, diced
2 sweet potatoes, thickly diced
1 white potato, thickly diced
1 tin of chopped tomatoes
2 tsp sundried tomato paste
2 tsp paprika
Handful of freshly chopped parsley
300ml vegetable stock
1 tin of butterbeans, drained

For the cobble/scone mix
100g self-raising flour
75ml natural yoghurt
2 tbsp olive oil
parsley

Macaroni Cheese

250g macaroni

25g butter

1 tbsp plain flour or
   cornflour

500–750ml milk

75–100g mature cheese
   (depending on your
   taste)

½ tsp mustard

Black pepper to taste

25g Parmesan cheese

This is one of those meals that simply satisfies – a real comfort food dish. You can prepare this in advance, but if you do, make the sauce a little runnier if you do as it does tend to thicken up when it's cold. You want a nice saucy macaroni cheese, not the type you slice!

1. Place the macaroni in boiling water and cook until tender. (The actual cooking time will depend on the type of macaroni you use, so refer to the manufacturer's instructions on the packet.)

2. Meanwhile, melt the butter gently in a saucepan on medium heat (not high!). Add the flour or cornflour and stir well with a wooden spoon. Add the milk, a little at a time, continuing to stir to avoid lumps.

3. Switch to a balloon whisk and continue to stir over a medium heat until the sauce begins to thicken. The balloon whisk will also help eradicate any lumps that may have materialised. Add more milk as necessary to get the desired thickness. The sauce should ideally be the thickness of custard.

4. Add the mature cheese and the mustard and stir well. Season with black pepper.

5. Drain the macaroni and combine this with the cheese sauce. Season to taste and pour into an ovenproof dish. (Remember to check that this fits well in your halogen oven.)

6. Preheat your halogen oven by using your preheat setting, or set the temperature at 220°C.

7. Grate the Parmesan cheese and sprinkle over the bake.

8. Place on the low rack and cook for 15 minutes until golden and bubbling.

Courgette and Pepper Pasta Bake

Ingredients:

Olive oil

3–4 courgettes, sliced

2 red peppers, thickly
   diced

200g penne pasta

3 tomatoes,
   chopped/diced

50g cooked broad beans
   or soya beans

1–2 tsp sundried tomato
   paste

200g cream cheese

200ml milk

50–75g mature cheddar,
   grated

This is a lovely dish, as roasting the peppers and courgettes creates much nicer flavour. You can adjust the cheddar to suit your taste – some like a cheesy topping, others prefer the lightness of a simply creamy sauce.

1. Place the courgettes and peppers in your ovenproof dish and drizzle with a little oil. Place on the high rack in the halogen. Set the temperature to 220°C and cook for 10–15 minutes.

2. Meanwhile, boil the water for the pasta and cook as per the manufacturer's instructions.

3. While they are both cooking, mix the cream cheese, milk and cheese together. Season to taste.

4. Remove the courgettes and peppers from the oven. Stir in the chopped tomatoes, broad beans and sundried tomato paste. Drain the pasta and stir this in with the vegetables.

5. Pour the cream cheese mixture over the top of the pasta and place back in the oven for 10 minutes.

6. Serve immediately.

Roasted Red Onion, Beetroot and Pepper Salad with Pine Nuts

Serves
4

Ingredients:
75g pine nuts
3 red onions, cut into
  wedges
2 beetroots, cut into
  wedges
2 red peppers, cut into
  wedges
Olive oil spray
Black pepper
Sea salt
Balsamic vinegar
Mixed salad leaves
2 tbsp extra virgin olive oil

A really lovely warm salad packed with goodness.

1. Place the pine nuts on a baking tray, spread out evenly. Place on the highest rack (the grill rack works the best for this) and set the temperature to its highest setting – you are grilling them! Roast for a couple of minutes until they start to brown. Be careful as they can catch very quickly so don't wander off! Remove and leave to one side.

2. Place the onion, beetroot and pepper on a baking tray, spray with olive oil, sprinkle with sea salt, black pepper and a drizzle of balsamic vinegar. Heat the oven to 200°C. Place on the low rack and bake for 20–30 minutes.

3. Mix 2 tablespoons of extra virgin olive oil with 1 tablespoon of balsamic vinegar. Mix well and season to taste.

4. Remove the roasted vegetables from the oven.

5. Place the salad leaves on your serving plates. Add the roasted vegetables, combining well.

6. Sprinkle with pine nuts and finish with a drizzle of the dressing.

7. Serve immediately.

Healthy Roasted Vegetable Pizza

Serves
2–4

For those who like healthier choices this is a great dish. It's also suitable for vegans as it does not contain cheese.

1. Sift the flour into a bowl.

2. Mix the water, yeast, sugar and oil together. Make sure the sugar is dissolved. Make a well in the middle of the flour and pour in the yeast mixture.

3. Mix thoroughly before transferring the dough onto a floured board. Knead well until the dough springs back when pulled.

4. Place the dough in a floured bowl and cover with cling film or a warm, damp cloth until it has doubled in size. This takes about 1 hour.

5. Place the vegetables in an ovenproof dish and drizzle with a little olive oil. Place on the high rack and cook for 15–20 minutes at 210°C until they are roasted. Remove and leave to one side until you are ready to make the pizza.

6. Knead again, and divide into individual pizza bases or as preferred.

7. Once your dough has proved, roll out to the desired thickness and size. Cover with a small layer of tomato pasta sauce or tomato purée. Add your roasted vegetables. Season to taste.

8. I normally place my pizza on a sheet of greased tinfoil and cook directly on the lower rack. You can buy tins with holes in which allow the base of pizzas or pies to brown.

9. Turn your halogen oven to 200°C and cook for 10–15 minutes.

10. Before serving sprinkle with a few basil leaves.

Ingredients:

For the dough
500g strong wholemeal or
    granary bread flour
325ml warm water
1 sachet of dried yeast
1 teaspoon brown sugar
2 tbsp olive oil

For the topping
2–3 tbsp pasta sauce or
    tomato purée
1 red onion, cut into
    wedges

1 pepper thickly sliced
1 courgette, thickly sliced
½ aubergine, thickly sliced
5–10 cherry tomatoes
5–8 olives
Olive oil
Basil leaves

Serves

4–6

Ingredients:

6 sheets of filo pastry

40g butter

250g feta cheese,
   crumbled

400g baby leaf spinach,
   roughly torn

50g toasted pine nuts

Grated nutmeg

Seasoning

Sesame or poppy seeds

Spinach and Feta Pie

Serve this with a selection of fresh salad dishes and new potatoes – the perfect dish for a summer's evening.

1. Melt the butter in a saucepan or place it in a bowl in your halogen oven to melt, though make sure this does not burn.

2. Layer three sheets of filo pastry in the base of your pie dish (make sure this fits comfortably within your halogen oven). Brush with butter between the sheets and allow the sheets to hang over the edge to give you enough to form the sides of the pie.

3. Place a thin layer of spinach leaves on top of the pastry, then add a layer of crumbled feta, seasoning with black pepper and nutmeg between the layers. Repeat this, finishing with the feta layer. You can add some toasted pine nuts for extra texture.

4. Cover with more filo sheets, again brushing each one with butter. Bring the edges of the pastry together to form a crust and remove any excess pastry around the edges.

5. Brush with butter and sprinkle with poppy or sesame seeds.

6. Set the temperature to 200°C.

7. Place on the low rack and bake for 30–40 minutes, until golden.

Roasted Pumpkin Soup

Serves
4–6

This makes a delicious treat for Halloween or, for an all-year treat, you can use other squash.

1. Cut the pumpkin, sweet potato and carrots into wedges. Place on a baking tray. Lightly brush with oil. Combine the garlic, onion and spices, and sprinkle over the vegetables.

2. Place on the low rack in the halogen oven, set the temperature to 200°C and bake for 20 minutes.

3. Remove the flesh from the pumpkin wedges, roughly chop the roasted vegetables and place in your casserole dish. Add all the remaining ingredients and combine well.

4. Place the casserole dish on the low rack. Cover with lid or with tinfoil secured tightly. Cook at 200°C for 30–40 minutes.

5. Cool slightly, and use an electric hand blender to purée until smooth. Season as required.

6. For impressive presentation, use hollowed out pumpkins as serving dishes.

Ingredients:

- 1 small pumpkin
- 1 medium sweet potato
- 1–2 carrots, thickly chopped
- Olive oil
- 1 onion, chopped
- 1–2 garlic cloves, crushed
- 1 tsp grated root ginger
- 1 tsp grated nutmeg
- 1 tsp ground coriander
- 2 sticks of celery , diced
- 4 tomatoes, peeled and chopped
- 2 tsp of tomato purée (optional)
- 300–425ml water or stock
- 15ml lemon juice
- Seasoning to taste

Quorn Bolognese Stuffed Tomatoes

Ingredients:

Spray of olive oil

1 red onion, finely
   chopped

1–3 cloves of garlic,
   crushed (depending on
   personal taste)

1 red pepper, diced

1 bag of quorn mince

50g chopped mushrooms

1 tin of tomatoes

2 tbsp sundried tomato
   purée

200ml low calorie red wine

1 tsp dried oregano

Few basil leaves (optional)

8 beef tomatoes (extra
   large tomatoes)

Olive oil

This recipe is perfect for using up any leftover bolognese sauce.
Or why not double up the bolognese recipe and make two dishes?

1. Spray a sauté pan with a little olive oil. Add the onion, garlic
and peppers and cook until they start to soften.

2. Add the quorn and cook for 5 minutes before adding the
mushrooms, tomatoes, tomato purée and wine.

3. Season to taste and add the oregano and basil leaves.

4. Leave to simmer gently for 10 minutes. Add a little water if it
starts to dry up.

5. Cut the tops off the beef tomatoes, keeping them to use as lids.
Scoop out the centre of the tomatoes – you can chop these and
add to your bolognese mixture. You will then be left with a tomato
shell and a lid.

6. When the bolognese mixture is ready, carefully fill the
tomatoes, but do not overfill them. Place the lid on top and place
the tomatoes on a baking tray (make sure this fits in your halogen
oven).

7. Spray with olive oil and season with sea salt and black pepper.
Place on the high rack and set the temperature to 190°C. Bake for
15–20 minutes.

8. Serve immediately with a lovely salad.

Mushroom and Cashew Nut Roast

Ingredients:

1 red onion finely chopped

200g cashew nuts
  (chopped)

250g mushrooms (I prefer
  chestnut but choose
  whatever works for you)

50g wholemeal or gluten
  free breadcrumbs

2 tsp yeast extract

This is made so much easier if you have a food processor that chops food. I can make this in minutes; otherwise you will drive yourself nuts (excuse the pun!) with all that chopping. I have many friends who are meat eaters and they all love this recipe.

1. Spray the sauté pan with a little olive oil and cook the onion until translucent.

2. Add nuts and mushrooms and cook for five minutes.

3. Add yeast extract, followed by the breadcrumbs, and cook for another few minutes.

4. Place into a lined loaf tin and press down to form a firm base.

5. Place on the low rack and set the temperature to 190°C. Bake in the oven for 30 minutes.

6. To add more pizzazz, why not serve with some roasted nuts on top.

7. NB: This dish can be frozen (before baking) and used when needed.

Roast Vegetable Pasta

Serves

4

This is a really healthy dish if you use wholewheat, spelt, vegetable or rice pasta.

1. Place the vegetables in a bowl. Add a drizzle of olive oil and dash of balsamic vinegar. Use your hands to mix together ensuring everything is evenly coated.

2. Tip this into your baking dish. Season to taste and add a few sprigs of thyme.

3. Place on the high rack. Set the temperature to 210°C and cook for 20–25 minutes.

4. Meanwhile, cook your pasta following your manufacturer's instructions. Do check your timings as it would be nice to have the pasta ready at the same time as the roasted vegetables.

5. Drain the pasta and mix in the roasted vegetables. Serve immediately.

Ingredients:

2 red onions, cut into
    wedges
2–3 cloves of garlic,
    roughly chopped
2 red peppers, thickly
    sliced
10–15 cherry tomatoes
2–3 courgettes, thickly
    sliced
Olive oil
Balsamic vinegar
Seasoning
2–3 sprigs of thyme
250–300g fusilli pasta

Vegetable Crumble

Spray of olive oil

1 red onion, finely
chopped

2–3 cloves of garlic,
roughly chopped

1 red pepper, sliced

1 green pepper, sliced

2 courgettes, sliced

½ aubergine, diced

1 sweet potato, diced

2–3 sprigs of thyme

1 tin of chopped tomatoes

1 tin of butterbeans,
drained

150ml water or low salt
vegetable stock

75g wholemeal flour

25g butter or low fat
margarine

40g oats

30g wholemeal
breadcrumbs

25g chopped peanuts

25g sunflower seeds

25g pumpkin seed

2 tbsp linseeds

This can be prepared in advance or frozen uncooked, ready to cook when needed. You can buy combined seed mix from supermarkets instead of the individual seeds if you prefer.

1. Chop all the vegetables (except the tomatoes and butterbeans) and place on a baking tray. Spray with a little olive oil and add a few sprigs of thyme.

2. Place on the high rack and set the temperature to to 200°C. Bake in the oven for 20 minutes.

3. While that is baking, you can prepare the crumble ingredients. Rub the flour with the margarine to form breadcrumbs.

4. Mix in the remaining ingredients (oats, peanuts, seeds and breadcrumbs), season to taste and leave to one side.

5. Remove the roasted vegetables from the oven. Place in your ovenproof dish, and stir in the chopped tomatoes, drained butterbeans and water or stock. Season to taste.

6. Cover with the crumble mix.

7. Place back in the oven on the high rack, turning the temperature down to 180°C and cook for 15–20 minutes.

8. Serve with a salad.

Celery and Blue Cheese Soup

Serves

4–6

This is a lovely soup with a fantastic flavour. You can cook this on the hob if you prefer, but it works equally well in the halogen as described below. Feel free to season to your taste. Why not serve with some delicious bruschetta made in the halogen?

1. In a casserole dish (make sure it fits in the halogen), add the onion, butter, celery and potato. Place on the high rack (or the low rack if your dish is too big to fit) and turn the temperature to 220°C. Cook for 5–8 minutes, stirring occasionally to distribute and help soften.

2. Add the water or stock. Cover with a lid or double thickness of tin foil (making sure this is secure) and continue to cook for 30 minutes.

3. Remove the lid and check to see if the diced vegetables are soft. Once soft you can add the blue cheese and season to taste. If you like a creamier soup, you can add a dollop or two of crème fraîche or thick Greek yoghurt, though personally I don't think it needs this. Liquidise or whizz with a stick blender until smooth.

4. Serve immediately or remove and leave to one side until needed. It does freeze well or keeps in an airtight container in the fridge for 2–3 days.

Ingredients:

1 white onion, finely chopped
25g butter
1 head of celery, finely diced
1 medium/large potato, finely diced
800ml–1 litre of hot water or hot vegetable stock (use low salt stock, as cheese is very salty)
150g blue cheese
Season to taste

Chapter 6
Desserts

Personally I think the best part of a meal is the pudding. It is foolish to expect me to restrain myself – puddings are meant to be enjoyed and I certainly do that! Here are some simple yet delicious recipes I hope you will enjoy as much as I have.

Queen of Puddings

Ingredients:

90g white bread, cubed

45g sugar

420ml milk

45g butter

1 tsp vanilla extract or
    paste

2 eggs, separated

60g caster sugar

3 tbsp jam (I use raspberry
    but feel free to use
    whatever you prefer)

My mum used to make this for us when we were children. Comforting puddings are making a well-earned revival; so much nicer than shop-bought processed puddings.

1. Grease your ovenproof dish.

2. Place your cubed bread in a bowl. Sprinkle with the sugar.

3. Heat the milk, vanilla extract and butter to almost boiling point and then pour over the bread and sugar mixture. When cool, add the egg yolks and whisk until combined well.

4. Pour this into your greased ovenproof dish. Place on the low rack and set the temperature to 180°C. Cook for 30–35 minutes until set.

5. Whilst this is cooking, beat your egg whites until they form soft peaks, adding half of the caster sugar gradually. Melt your jam on low heat as you don't want to burn this.

6. Spread the jam over the set mixture. Top this with your whisked egg whites. Sprinkle with the remaining caster sugar.

7. Place back in the oven and cook for another 8–10 minutes until golden.

Rhubarb Crumble

Serves
4–6

I love rhubarb! There's nothing nicer than picking rhubarb fresh from the garden and making this delicious dessert. Serve with vanilla ice-cream.

Ingredients:
650g rhubarb
50g sugar (or to taste)
50–100ml water
200g plain flour
30g ground almonds
30g oatmeal
100g butter
50g brown sugar

1. Place your rhubarb in a saucepan and add the sugar and water. Cook gently for 5–8 minutes to help start to soften the fruit.

2. Pour this into your ovenproof dish. (Remember to make sure the dish fits well in your halogen oven.)

3. In a bowl, combine the flour, ground almonds and oatmeal. Add the butter and rub until it forms a texture similar to breadcrumbs. Add the brown sugar and combine well.

4. Pour this over the fruit base, making sure it is spread evenly.

5. Place the crumble on the low rack and cook for 20 minutes at 190°C.

6. Serve with a dollop of vanilla ice-cream.

Variation

You can use different fruit in this recipe – just go for whichever fruit you prefer! To make a traditional apple crumble, use 750g of apples, sliced or diced (I use Bramley apples, which have a good flavour). Add the sugar and water as for the rhubarb recipe, and cook gently for 10 minutes to soften the fruit. I prefer to have my apples with a bit of bite to them rather than a purée. Serve this with lovely home-made custard.

Bread and Butter Pudding

4–6 slices of white bread
  (stale is ideal)

30g butter

60g sultanas

50g sugar

2 tsp of ground cinnamon

2 eggs, beaten

300ml milk

75ml cream (optional –
  you can increase the
  milk quantity to 375ml if
  you prefer; whole milk is
  creamier)

This is one of my absolute favourite comfort puddings. You can opt to use cream if you are not particularly worried about the calorific value of the pudding.

1. Grease your ovenproof dish with butter. Butter your bread slices and line the dish, sprinkling chopped sultanas, sugar and cinnamon between the slices.

2. In a jug, mix the eggs, milk and cream (if used) together. Pour this over the bread mixture, pushing the bread down into the liquid where necessary. I then let this sit for about ten minutes to absorb the milk.

3. Preheat the halogen oven using your preheat setting, or turn the temperature to 190°C.

4. Push the bread down into the liquid, sprinkle with more cinnamon if you like the flavour and place the dish on the low rack of the halogen oven.

5. Cook for 30 minutes until the top is golden.

Baked Cinnamon Apples

Serves

4

A traditional autumnal treat that is really easy to prepare. Serve with ice-cream, custard or a healthy dollop of low fat Greek yoghurt.

Ingredients:

4 Bramley apples, cored
    but not peeled
2 tsp runny honey
2–3 tsp ground cinnamon
Sultanas
Brown sugar

1. Preheat the halogen oven using the preheat setting or set the temperature to 220°C.

2. Wash and core your apples, leaving the skins intact. Mix the honey with 10ml of boiling water and the cinnamon. Stir until dissolved.

3. Place the apples on a baking tray or ovenproof dish and add two tablespoons of water to the dish. Brush the apples with the honey mixture.

4. Stuff the cores of the apples with sultanas. Finish with a sprinkling of brown sugar.

5. Bake in the oven on the low rack for 20–30 minutes until soft.

6. Serve with low fat crème fraîche or natural yoghurt.

Gooey Chocolate Puddings

Serves

4

These are baked in little ramekin dishes. If you turn them out of the dishes immediately they are cooked, they will droop and ooze out chocolate when punctured with a spoon, but that is the general appeal. Serve with a dollop of crème fraîche and a few fresh raspberries for the perfect indulgent pud!

Ingredients:

350g dark chocolate

150g sugar

60g butter

4 eggs

2 tsp vanilla extract

2 tsp chocolate extract
   (optional)

60g plain flour

1. Melt your chocolate using a bain-marie or a bowl over a saucepan of hot water (don't let the bottom of the bowl touch the water!). Once melted, leave to one side.

2. Meanwhile combine the butter and sugar and beat until light and fluffy. Add the eggs, vanilla and chocolate extract. Combine well before folding in the sifted flour.

3. Finally add the melted chocolate and combine well.

4. Preheat the halogen oven using the preheat setting, or set the temperature to 200°C.

5. Thoroughly grease your ramekin dishes and dust with flour. Pour in the mixture and place on the low rack.

6. Cook for 12–15 minutes.

7. Turn onto a serving plate. For those who like an extra chocolate hit, drizzle with more chocolate and serve with a dollop of crème fraîche – delicious!

Cheat's Treacle Tart

Ingredients:

1 ready-made pastry case

300g golden syrup

25g butter

50ml double cream
(optional)

2 eggs, beaten

100–150g breadcrumbs

If you love treacle tart, why not try this simple recipe? Using pre-baked pastry cases saves time and avoids soggy bottom pastry! This recipe is perfect for the 7–8inch pastry case found in supermarkets.

1. In a saucepan, gently heat the golden syrup until it becomes runny. Add the butter and stir well. Add the cream (if using), and the beaten egg and combine well.

2. Add the breadcrumbs and stir well. You want a fluid consistency, not thick and lumpy, but with enough texture to give the golden syrup body.

3. Pour this into your pastry case.

4. Set the temperature to 170°C. Place the tart on the high rack and cook for 30 minutes. If it is not quite cooked at this point, turn the temperature down to 150°C and check it at 5 minute intervals, taking care to avoid burning. The pie should be firm and golden.

5. Serve with a dollop of cream, crème fraîche or natural yoghurt.

Simple Nutty Pear and Chocolate Crumble

Serves
4–6

Ingredients:
2–3 tins of pears (in
  natural juice), diced
75g dark chocolate chips
  or thick chunks (I prefer
  using thick chunks of
  chocolate)
200g granola (I use plain
  granola without the
  added fruit but feel free
  to use what you prefer)

I love this recipe – it is quick and so very easy. It uses up store-cupboard ingredients and is perfect with fresh pears, but for simplicity in this recipe I use tinned. If you don't have granola, you could use muesli. Serve with a dollop of crème fraîche.

1. Drain the pears, before chopping into chunks. Place in your ovenproof dish. Add a little of the drained juice – just enough to prevent the pears drying out.

2. Stir in the chocolate chips or chunks.

3. Sprinkle the granola over the pears.

4. Place on the low rack and bake at 190°C for 15 minutes.

5. Serve immediately with a dollop of crème fraîche.

Plum Crumble

10–12 plums, stoned and
  sliced

100g sugar (or to taste)

50ml water

Juice of ½ lemon

200g plain flour

75g oats

100g butter

75g brown sugar

Zest of lemon

Plums are packed with phytonutrients. This crumble is delicious, but you may need to adjust the sweetness to suit your own taste. If you want to avoid sugar, why not try xylitol or stevia (natural sugar alternatives not to be confused with artificial sweeteners!).

1. Place the plums in a saucepan and add the sugar, water and lemon juice. Cook gently for 10 minutes to help start to soften the fruit.

2. Pour this into your ovenproof dish, making sure it fits well in your halogen oven.

3. In a bowl, combine the flour and oats. Add the butter and rub until it forms a texture similar to breadcrumbs. Add the sugar and lemon zest and combine well.

4. Pour this over the fruit base, making sure it is spread evenly.

5. Place the crumble on the low rack and cook for 20 minutes at 190°C.

6. Serve with a dollop of home-made custard.

Lemon Tart

Serves

6–8

I love lemon tart and this recipe is so simple anyone can make it. You can cheat and use a pre-baked pastry case or ready to roll sweet shortcrust pasty, or simply follow the recipe from scratch. This recipe uses 4 egg yolks so why not use the leftover egg whites to make a meringue for a Pavlova or Eton Mess?

1. Place the flour and icing sugar in a bowl and combine well. Rub in the butter until the mixture resembles breadcrumbs. Combine with the egg yolk and a little water if necessary until you have a firm dough. Place this dough in the fridge to rest for 5–10 minutes.

2. Once rested, line a flan tin with your pastry. Prick with a fork and place a sheet of baking parchment over the top. You can add baking beans if you wish to prevent the pastry from rising.

3. Preheat your halogen oven using the preheat setting, or set the temperature to 190°C.

4. Place the flan on the low rack and cook for 10–15 minutes until baked.

5. Whilst this is cooking you can prepare the filling by mixing the condensed milk, zest and juice of the lemons and the egg yolks together. Mix thoroughly.

6. Pour this mixture onto your pastry base and place back in the halogen oven. Cook for another 10–12 minutes.

7. Remove and leave to cool. Sprinkle with icing sugar before serving.

Ingredients:

For the pastry
100g plain flour
40g icing sugar
50g butter
1 egg yolk

For the filling
1 400g tin of condensed milk
Juice and zest of 3 lemons
3 egg yolks

Winter Spice Crumble

600g chopped fruit (I use
  rhubarb, Bramley apples
  and plums)
75g sugar
100ml red wine
75ml orange juice
3 tsp cinnamon
1 tsp allspice
200g plain flour
75g oats
1 tsp mixed spice
100g butter
75g brown sugar

If you love the flavour of cinnamon and allspice, this is the pudding for you. Serve with vanilla ice-cream.

1. Preheat the halogen oven using the preheat settings, or set the temperature to 180°C.

2. Place your fruit in a saucepan and add the sugar, orange juice and wine. Cook gently for 5–8 minutes to help start to soften the fruit.

3. Mix in the spices and stir well, pressing the fruit a little with your spoon to help break/soften.

4. Pour this into your ovenproof dish, making sure it fits well in your halogen oven.

5. In a bowl, combine the flour, oats and mixed spice. Add the butter and rub until it forms a texture similar to breadcrumbs. Add the sugar and combine well.

6. Pour this over the fruit base, making sure it is spread evenly.

7. Place the crumble on the low rack and cook for 20 minutes.

8. Serve with a dollop of home-made custard.

Peach Melba Delight

Serves
4–6

This is another favourite in our house. It is similar to the Vanilla and Blueberry Brûlée. You can use fresh peaches when in season, or if you are in hurry, tinned peaches in their own juice could be used.

- 200g raspberries, frozen or fresh
- 1 tbsp sugar
- 2–3 ripe peaches (or you could use tinned ones)
- 350–400g Greek yoghurt
- 3 tbsp low fat crème fraîche
- 1 tsp vanilla paste
- 3–4 tbsp brown sugar

1. In your ovenproof dish, place the frozen or fresh raspberries and sprinkle with a tablespoon of sugar. Place on the low rack and cook for 5 minutes at 180°C to soften.

2. Remove and crush. If you do not want the pips, you could put this through a sieve to form a finer raspberry purée rather than a mush.

3. In a bowl, mix the yoghurt and crème fraîche together with the vanilla paste.

4. Place the sliced peaches in the bottom of your ovenproof serving dish. Drizzle with two-thirds of the raspberry purée.

5. In the bowl of crème fraîche, add the remaining raspberry purée and fold to create a ripple effect – don't over stir.

6. Pour this onto the peaches and smooth to form an even coating.

7. Cover this with a generous coating of brown sugar.

8. Place on the high rack for 3–4 minutes at 250°C. Watch this constantly, ensuring you are ready to remove before it burns!

9. Serve hot or cold.

Lemon Saucy Pudding

Ingredients:

50g butter

150g sugar

Juice and zest of 2 large
   or 3 medium lemons

4 medium eggs (or 3
   large), separated

1 tsp vanilla essence or
   paste

300ml milk

50g plain flour

This is a really light pudding that is quite addictive. The soufflé-like sponge sits on top of a zingy lemon sauce. Delicious!

1. Beat the butter and sugar together until creamy.

2. Using a sharp vegetable peeler, peel the zest from 2-3 lemons (depending on desired lemony intensity). The peeler magically peels the zest and leaves the white pith behind. Finely chop the zest and add to the beaten sugar/butter mixture.

3. Add the egg yolks, vanilla and lemon juice. Beat well before adding the flour and milk.

4. This will form a quite runny batter. Give it a thorough stir to make sure the mixer has not left anything on the edges.

5. Meanwhile, in a clean bowl, beat the egg whites until they form soft peaks.

6. Fold this into the batter gently.

7. Grease your baking dish with butter. I use a Pyrex baking dish but you could use individual ramekin dishes (see below). Pour in the mixture.

8. Using the bowl of your halogen oven, pour in hot water to a depeth of approximately 3cm (2 inches).

9. Place your baking tray in the water to create a bain-marie. If you prefer and have room, you can place a baking tray filled with water on the lower rack and add small ramekin dishes filled with the mixture.

10. Turn the halogen oven to 150°C and cook for 40–45 minutes

(20–30 minutes for individual ramekin dishes). The pudding should have a golden sponge topping which is firm to touch.

11. When you serve the pudding, you will notice the bottom half is a gooey lemon sauce and the top should be a lovely light sponge.

12. Serve with crème fraîche or Greek yoghurt.

Mulled Baked Pears

Ingredients:

4–6 ripe pears

400–500ml mulled wine

1 orange, thickly sliced

175g sugar

This can be prepared in advance. Serve with vanilla ice-cream or a dollop of crème fraîche.

1. Place the wine in a saucepan and heat up gently. Add half the sugar and stir until dissolved.

2. Peel your pears, retaining the stalk if possible. Cut the bottom off the pear allowing it to stand without falling over.

3. Place the orange slices in the bottom of your ovenproof dish. (The smaller the dish, the more of the pear will be covered in wine).

4. Place the pears in the dish. (You can sit the pears on top of the orange slices or lie flat to allow more of the pears to be covered in the liquid.)

5. Pour the wine over the pears. Sprinkle the pears with the remainder of the sugar.

6. Cover securely with foil and place on the low rack. Set the temperature to 160°C and cook for 45 minutes.

7. Uncover and spoon the wine back over the pears. Add more wine or red grape juice if necessary.

8. Cook uncovered for another 20 minutes or until the pears are soft.

9. Place the pears on a plate and drizzle over with the juice. Serve with a dollop of cream, Greek yoghurt or crème fraîche.

Boozy Plums

Serves
4–6

This is a perfect dinner party dessert. You can make it as boozy as you like, but offset the alcoholic taste with some creamy vanilla ice-cream or cream.

1. Preheat the halogen oven using the preheat setting, or set the temperature to 150°C.

2. Place the halved/stoned plums on a non-stick baking tray or ovenproof dish.

3. Drizzle over the honey and sprinkle with a little sugar. Add the port and water before placing on the low rack and cooking for 30–40 minutes until the plums are soft.

4. Remove and serve in individual bowls. Sprinkle with icing sugar and serve with some Amaretti biscuits.

Ingredients:

750g plums, halved, with
   stones removed
1–2 tbsp runny honey
75g sugar
100ml pink port
50ml water
Amaretti biscuits
Icing sugar

Chocolate Saucy Pudding

Serves
4–6

My mum used to make this when we were children and I rediscovered the recipe when I pinched her personal cookery notebook. We used to call this a magic pudding as the sauce is poured over the top of the cake, but during cooking it miraculously goes to the bottom. I have adapted the recipe to suit the halogen oven and it works really well. You could make this in small ramekin dishes, but adjust the cooking time for this.

1. In your mixer, beat the sugar and butter together until creamy and fluffy. Gradually add the beaten eggs, milk and vanilla and mix well before adding the flour and cocoa.

2. Pour into a greased ovenproof dish (or individual ramekin dishes) and smooth over until flat.

3. In bowl or jug, mix the boiling water, sugar and cocoa together and stir thoroughly until dissolved and lump free. Pour this over the sponge mixture.

4. Preheat your halogen oven using your preheat setting, or set the temperature to 175°C.

5. Place on the low rack and cook for 40–50 minutes, until the sponge is firm to touch.

6. Serve with a dollop of Greek yoghurt or crème fraîche and enjoy!

Ingredients:

115g sugar

115g butter

2 eggs, beaten

2 tbsp milk

1 tbsp vanilla essence or
   paste

100g self-raising flour

2 tbsp cocoa

300ml boiling water

2 tbsp sugar

1 tbsp cocoa

French Apple Tart

Ingredients:

For the pastry
150g plain flour
75g butter
75g sugar
1 egg, beaten
1 tbsp water

For the filling
1kg cooking apples
Lemon juice
15g butter
60g sugar
1–2 tsp cinnamon
3 tbsp apricot jam

This is a lovely dish. The recipe includes how to make the pastry case, but if you aren't up to making your own, you could buy ready-made sweet or puff pastry, or ready-cooked pastry cases. (These will obviously be more expensive than making your own.) Remember sometimes the halogen struggles to cook the base of a pie, so always make sure this is cooked before you remove it from the oven, and don't make the base pastry too thick. I have a pizza tray which has holes in the base. I often use this to make a free-style pie or transfer the almost cooked pie onto this if the base is not quite done. If in doubt, buy a ready-made case.

1. To make your pastry, place the flour in a bowl. Add the butter and rub to form a texture similar to breadcrumbs. Add the sugar and combine well.

2. Add the beaten egg and 1 tablespoon of water and combine until it forms a dough. Once formed, place this in the fridge to rest while you continue with the rest of the recipe.

3. Peel and thinly slice the apples and place them in water with a little lemon juice.

4. Preheat your halogen oven using the preheat setting, or set the temperature to 200°C.

5. Roll out the pastry and line your flan dish (make sure this fits in your halogen oven). Prick with a fork and place on the low rack of the oven for 15 minutes (cooking blind). You can use baking beans over a sheet of baking parchment if you want to prevent air bubbles in the pastry.

6. Whilst that is cooking, remove a third of the apple slices and place in a pan to soften with a little butter, a drizzle of water and a dessertspoonful of sugar. Stir until soft before adding almost all the cinnamon.

7. Remove the pastry case and smooth on the puréed apple. Over the top of this, place the apple slices in a nice even pattern, fanning out and overlapping slightly around the flan dish. Sprinkle with sugar and the remaining cinnamon.

8. Return to the low rack and bake for 25 minutes until the apples are cooked. Remove from the oven.

9. Gently heat the apricot jam, stirring continuously to avoid burning. Once this is runny, brush over the baked apples ensuring the top is well covered.

10. Serve hot or cold with ice-cream, crème fraîche or just on its own.

Vanilla and Blueberry Brûlée

Serves

4

I love all flavours of brulee - they are really simple to make. If you don't have blueberries you could swap for raspberries or a handful of summer fruits.

Ingredients:
150g blueberries
300ml 0% fat natural
    Greek yoghurt
1 tsp vanilla paste
4 egg yolks
1 tbsp cornflour
4 tbsp brown sugar

1. Place the blueberries in the base of each of four ramekin dishes.

2. Combine the yoghurt, vanilla paste, egg yolks and cornflour together – I use my hand blender for this.

3. Pour this mixture into each of the ramekin dishes.

4. Boil the kettle as you need hot water.

5. Place the ramekin dishes in the base of your halogen oven.

6. Carefully pour boiling water around the edges of the ramekin dishes until it is about halfway up the sides.

7. Set the temperature to 180°C and bake for 30 minutes. Remove and leave to cool. I normally leave these in the fridge for 30 minutes before serving.

8. When ready to serve, sprinkle with brown sugar. Place on the highest rack, making sure the dishes don't touch the element. Set the temperature to high (as if you are grilling) and caramelise the top until it is golden. Don't walk away from this as it will burn really quickly!

9. Serve immediately.

Fresh Berry Fruit Tart

For the pastry

325g plain flour

125g butter

100g icing sugar or caster
  sugar

1 whole egg

1 egg yolk

For the filling

75g tbsp cream cheese

2 tbsp lemon curd

approx. 250g selection of
  berries (raspberries,
  strawberries, blueberries,
  redcurrants, etc.)

Quick Jel jelly, red (I use
  Green's)

I adore any dessert with fresh berries. This recipe is quite simple to make but looks really impressive, and is perfect for a dinner party. For this recipe you will need a loose-bottom flan tin of approx. 23cm diameter.

1. Use a food processor to make the pastry as it avoids you handling it too much. Place the flour, sugar and butter in the processor and whizz.

2. Add the whole egg and egg yolk and whizz to form a dough ball.

3. Remove and place in a freezer bag and pop in the fridge to cool for at least 20 minutes.

4. When ready to use, roll out carefully, avoiding handling it too much, and line your tin.

5. Place a piece of greaseproof paper over the pastry and fill with baking beans (if you don't have baking beans you can use dried beans or rice).

6. Place on the high rack and cook at 210°C for 10 minutes.

7. Remove from the oven and remove the baking beans and greaseproof paper. Place back on the high rack and cook until the pastry is completely cooked – this should be another 10–15 minutes.

8. When the pastry is cool, you can start to fill.

9. Mix the cream cheese and lemon curd together. Spread this over the base of the pastry case.

10. Arrange the fruit on top.

11. Follow the Quick Jel instructions and pour this over the fruit. Place in the fridge to set (this usually takes no more than 20 minutes).

12. Serve and enjoy!

Chapter 7

Cakes, biscuits and treats

I often get asked if we can make cakes and biscuits in the halogen and the answer is always an enthusiastic yes! I love baking and I saw no reason why we could not adapt recipes to suit the halogen. As with all baking, there are many things that can affect the quality of the cake so in the following pages you will find some baking advice – please read this as it will really help you. My son started baking with me when he was a toddler. At 9 years old, he is now confident enough to make his own fairy cakes and always chooses to use the halogen as he likes watching them cook.

If you are nervous about cakes, I would suggest you follow his lead and try the basic sponge fairy cakes first. Larger cakes need to be tested before you take them out of the oven – cake times do vary due to machine variations and sizes, so sometimes you may find you have to cook for longer on a lower temperature for larger cakes.

Top Baking Tips

Here is a collection of tips that I hope will help save you time or help with your baking experience.

Read!

Always read the recipe right through before you start. Not only does this familiarise you with what you have to do, but also gives you time to check your ingredients, equipment and prepare your timings. There is no point starting a recipe, getting to the middle bit and finding out either that you have to soak something overnight before you proceed to the next step, or you don't have a key ingredient – I know, I have been that idiot!

Preparing your cake tins

I cannot emphasise enough the importance of lining/greasing your cake tins thoroughly before baking. I am a recent convert to cake tin liners. You can buy them for very little money from your local supermarket or cake store and they are well worth the investment. You can also buy reusable baking sheets which are great, but remember that most will be made to fit conventional ovens so you will have to make adjustments or seek alternatives for your halogen oven.

If you want to line tins yourself, you can butter the tin and then sprinkle with a coating of flour to make it non-stick. Alternatively, you can use baking parchment cut to size, though this will also have to be placed into a buttered tin.

Cooling racks

It is really important to cool cakes, biscuits or breads on a cooling rack, allowing the air to circulate all around. Cooling racks (also known as wire racks) are relatively cheap to buy, but if you don't have one, you could use your grill rack off your grill tray. Most cakes need to cool for up to 5 minutes in their tins before you turn them out onto the racks.

Mixing

Don't over or under mix – I know this sounds difficult, but you will get used to this. Creaming the butter and sugar together until light and fluffy takes only a minute or two in a food mixer. I personally still fold in the flour by hand, but that is force of habit. Over-mixing the flour can create a tough or rather solid cake. One great example of over-mixing is when thickening double cream. Stop when it gets to light peaks, as once it has been over-whipped, it will go lumpy and horrible.

Pastry

Pastry loves to be cold. Use cold butter (or even frozen), and don't handle the dough too much. A food processor makes light work of pastry. I always leave my dough in the fridge for at least 10 minutes before using – not only does this keep the pastry cool, it also helps avoid shrinkage when rolling out or baking as this time has allowed the pastry to relax.

Cake-making tips

You may follow a recipe exactly but your cake decides not to come out exactly as the celebrity chef does it – why does this happen? Well, with cake baking, there are so many things that can affect the end result – even down to simple changes in the temperature of your halogen oven (yes, there has been lots of feedback stating certain machines can be as much as 30°C out!). Here are some basic tips to help.

A doughy cake is often caused by too little rising agent, unsifted flour or not baking for long enough or at the right temperature to allow the cake to rise.

A heavy cake can be caused by not mixing (adding enough air to the mixture) correctly, not sifting the flour, not using enough rising agent or too much flour.

A dry cake tends to be overcooked or maybe the mixture did not have enough butter or wet ingredients in it. If you keep having this happen, check your timings. If you have dry fruit cakes, try grating a carrot, apple or even a mashed banana into the mixture, as this will help to moisten the cake.

Fruit sunk to the bottom of the cake is mainly caused by adding the fruit before the main sponge cake is mixed (i.e., cream the butter and sugar, add the beaten eggs, and then the sifted flour, before adding the fruit mixture). You may not have combined the fruit well enough, or simply made the cake mix too thin so it could not hold the additional ingredients.

Sunken cakes are normally caused by those impatient souls who can't resist opening the oven doors every few minutes 'just to check'. That's what glass doors are for! You may also have had too much liquid in your cake mix.

Burnt top, uncooked middle – If this happens, your oven temperature is too hot – turn the temperature down and cook for longer. Ignore those friendly hints of using tin foil in order to convince the cake to cook quicker as you will not get the right results. Remember, you can't rush perfection!

Cracked top – This probably means that your oven is too hot, so turn the temperature down and cook for a little longer. An uneven surface (with one side risen and the other low) can indicate uneven temperature.

Preheat your oven – I know the halogen appears not to require this, but old habits die hard and I prefer to preheat and know that when my cake enters the oven, the cake starts cooking immediately and does not get confused by rising temperatures.

When things go wrong

Don't panic if things go wrong – it happens. When I was learning how to cook at school, we were told to weigh our eggs, always to use butter, and the only flour available was either self-raising or plain. Now we never use the weight of the eggs to measure the other ingredients, as this can cause a mixture to be too wet or too dry. Flour quality varies so much now, too. I recently started using high grade sponge flour, which does make very light cakes but it does make the mixture wetter, and some cases I have had to increase the flour quantity for the recipe. Margarine can also cause problems with your cake mixture – some are better than others, I use Stork or butter.

When using the halogen oven remember that temperature fluctuations can occur. If you suspect this then test the temperature with an oven thermometer.

If the cake is too near the element it will burn quickly on the top so either use a height extension ring or place on the low rack.

If the cake seems to be cooking quickly on top but the middle/bottom is still raw, lower the temperature and cook for longer. I often cook larger cakes for 45+ minutes, especially fruit cakes or apple cake.

Always test the cake to see if it is cooked before you turn the cake out – there is nothing more upsetting than turning out a cake and finding the bottom is not cooked. Place a skewer or sharp knife into the centre of the cake. If it comes out clean, the cake is cooked.

Cookies and biscuits

Don't over mix cookies or biscuits as this could result in tough biscuits. Also remember that biscuits and cookies harden once cooled so avoid overcooking unless you want to break your teeth on them!

Butter icing

When mixing icing sugar, you may end up in a white cloud of dust if you are not careful. Don't

be too over generous with the icing sugar at first. Add a little at a time – yes, it may take longer but you will avoid the dust cloud and remain in control.

Chocolate

When melting chocolate, use a bain-marie or place a heatproof bowl over a pan of boiling water. Be careful not to let the water touch the bottom of the bowl as this will result in thick and unusable chocolate. When a recipe asks for chocolate, try to use the best quality you can. Some cheap cooking chocolate is so far removed from the real thing – over sweet and not really that nice. I prefer to use dark chocolate with at least 70% cocoa content. I also buy as a special treat (and it lasts for ages), Willie Harcourt's Pure Cacao (£5.99 from Waitrose or visit www.williescacao.com for some great in savoury and sweet recipes). I am a huge fan, even more so as it is actually a very healthy product. Chocolate and healthy – my type of food!

Lemons and limes

You may be familiar with this scenario – you need the juice of a lemon or lime, but it just seems so difficult to squeeze out the juice. A top tip is to warm the lemon or lime gently first. Once warm, they will release their juice with ease.

Finish with style

You have made a cake or dish that tastes wonderful but maybe lacks kerb appeal – well, learn to finish with style! You can add a sprinkle of icing sugar or cocoa sifted over the top of a cake, or spread it with butter icing and top with fresh fruit. A glaze of dried fruit and nuts can tastefully cover the top of your fruit cake, or you can even grab some fondant icing and let your inner child free to create (remember Play-Doh?). Don't despair if things go a bit awry when you first start baking, as it really is a learning process. Remember, tasty cakes come in all shapes and sizes and if you are baking for your children, they simply won't care – 'Just give me the cake!'

Ingredients:

2 eggs, beaten

175g golden sugar

250ml natural yoghurt

1 tsp vanilla extract

300g self-raising flour

175g blueberries

Blueberry Muffins

Forget the high fat, calorie-laden blueberry muffins you find in coffee shops – make your own! They are delicious and much healthier. If you are on a wheat- or gluten-free diet, swap the flour for Doves Farm gluten and wheat-free self-raising and add 30ml of water to the mixture.

1. Preheat your halogen cooker using your preheat setting, or set the temperature to 190°C.

2. Beat the sugar and eggs together until fluffy. Add the yoghurt and vanilla extract and beat again.

3. Sift the flour into the mixture and carefully fold into the mix. When thoroughly mixed, add the blueberries.

4. Place in cupcake or muffin cases in a muffin/cupcake tray. I have not been able to find a round muffin tray so I use silicon muffin cases and place these on the baking trays that come with the halogen oven accessory packs. You can comfortably fit 10 on the tray – though this mixture will make 6 large ones.

5. Place on the low rack and cook for 12–18 minutes. The cakes should be firm and spring back when touched.

6. Cool the muffins on your cooling rack before serving.

Apple and Almond Crumble Cake

This is one of my favourite cakes. It is very soft and fluffy when cooked. Placed in an airtight container it will keep for 2–3 days – not as long as other cakes, but to be honest it always gets eaten before then anyway!

1. Preheat the halogen oven to 160°C, and line an 18cm cake tin (I use a springform tin with a cake liner).

2. Cream the sugar and butter until light and fluffy, before adding 2 eggs. Beat well.

3. Peel and chop two Bramley apples into chunks and add to the mixture, along with 1 teaspoon of almond essence.

4. Fold in the self-raising flour. Pour half the mixture into your lined springform tin.

5. Peel half a Bramley apple and cut into slices. Place the slices over the mixture.

6. Top with the remaining cake mix and finish with a few random apple slices.

7. In a bowl mix the plain flour, ground almonds and sugar with the butter. Sprinkle this over the cake.

8. Pop on the low rack and cook for 50 minutes. If it starts to go brown, use a height extension ring or cover with foil. Test the cake by placing a skewer or cake tester into the centre of the cake. If it comes out clean the cake is done. It may need longer, as cooking time can depend on the machine, so continue to test at 5–10 minute intervals until the skewer comes out clean.

9. Cool on a rack before devouring! This cake is delicious hot or cold – it's a light, moist cake so ideally consume it within a day or two.

Ingredients:
170g sugar
120g butter
2 eggs
3 Bramley apples, peeled and sliced
1 tsp almond essence
240g self-raising flour
50g plain flour
20g ground almonds
40g butter
20g brown sugar

Apple Turnovers

Ingredients:

Half a pack of puff pastry

Stewed apple, or 2
   cooking apples, cut into
   fine slices

Beaten egg or milk

Brown sugar to sprinkle

These are great if you have any spare puff pastry or stewed apple to use up. Stewed apple is easiest, but you can simply slice some cooking apples into the centre of the pastry, add some sugar and off you go.

1. Preheat your halogen oven using the preheat setting, or turn the temperature to 200°C.

2. Roll out the puff pastry to about 4–5mm thick. Cut into squares, approximately 15–22cm (6–8 inches) square.

3. Place 2–3 teaspoons of stewed apple or apple slices in the centre of the puff pastry squares. If using apple slices, add a sprinkle of sugar and cinnamon to taste.

4. Using a pastry brush, brush the milk or egg around the edges of the square. I normally fold diagonally to form a triangle. Secure the edges by crimping.

5. Coat with milk or egg and sprinkle with brown sugar.

6. Place on the low rack and bake for 15–18 minutes until golden.

Scones

Makes

4–8 (depending on size of cases)

Ingredients:
250g self raising flour
50g butter
50g caster sugar
100ml buttermilk
1 egg

As I am from Devon, I really needed to include the traditional scones served with cream and home-made jam – let's not argue about who puts the cream or jam first (I am a cream then jam person)… Whichever way round you do it, no one can complain about the taste. This recipe uses buttermilk and an egg. I used this recipe to teach 5–9 year olds, and even with their constant handling, the scones still came out brilliantly, so really, this is proven to be child's-play. If you are on a wheat or gluten free diet, swap the flour for Doves Farm gluten and wheat-free self-raising and add 30ml of milk to the mixture.

1. Preheat your halogen oven using the preheat setting, or set the temperature to 210°C.

2. Sift the flour into a bowl. Add the butter and rub until the mixture resembles breadcrumbs. Add the sugar and combine well.

3. Mix the buttermilk with the egg and add this to the flour mixture. Combine to form a firm, but not wet, dough.

4. Place this on a floured board, and press out until 3–4cm thick. Cut with a pastry cutter and place on your greased baking tray. Brush with a beaten egg (this gives a lovely golden colour to the scones).

5. Place in the halogen oven for 10–12 minutes.

6. Place on a cooling rack or serve warm!

Ingredients:

175g butter

175g sugar

3 eggs, beaten

175g self-raising flour

75g fresh raspberries

50g white chocolate chips

White Chocolate and Raspberry Cupcakes

These are my dad's favourite cupcakes – they really are yummy. Use fresh raspberries, as frozen ones make the mixture too wet. If you are on a wheat- or gluten-free diet, swap the flour for Doves Farm gluten- and wheat-free self-raising and add 30ml of water to the mixture.

1. Preheat the halogen oven using the preheat setting, or set to 200°C.

2. Cream the butter and sugar together until pale and fluffy.

3. Add the eggs a little at a time and continue to beat well.

4. Sift the flour and fold into the mixture gently.

5. When thoroughly mixed, add the raspberries and chocolate chips and combine.

6. Place in cupcake or muffin cases in a muffin/cupcake tray. I have not been able to find a round muffin tray so I use silicon muffin cases and place these on the baking trays that come with the halogen oven accessory packs. You can comfortably fit 10 on the tray. This mixture should make 6–12 cakes depending on their size.

7. Place on the low rack and cook for 12–18 minutes. The cakes should be firm and spring back when touched.

8. Place on a cooling rack to cool.

Chocolate Brownies

Makes
10–12 (depending on size cut)

Ingredients:
225g butter
150g dark chocolate
225g self-raising flour
125g brown sugar
4 eggs
60g chopped hazelnuts
75g dark chocolate chips

I have small square trays that fit in my halogen but if you don't have these you can still make the brownies in round tins – they will taste the same, just in a different shape! If you are on a wheat or gluten free diet, swap the flour for Doves Farm gluten and wheat free self-raising and add 30ml of water to the mixture.

1. Place the butter and chocolate in a pan and melt gently on a low heat.

2. Meanwhile sift the flour into a bowl. Add the sugar, hazelnuts and chocolate chips. Combine well.

3. Remove the chocolate from the heat. Beat the eggs and add them to the chocolate mix before quickly adding to the flour mixture and combining well.

4. Place the mixture into your lined tin (the size will depend on your halogen oven, but I use an 22cm square tin).

5. Place on the low rack. Set the temperature to 190°C and cook for 25–35 minutes. Test to see if it is cooked by inserting a skewer into the centre of the cake. If it comes out clean it is cooked. If it is wet place back in the oven and check every 5 minutes.

6. Remove and leave to cool before cutting into squares.

Cheating Cheesy Straws

Ingredients:

1 packet of puff pastry
100g mature Cheddar,
   grated
Handful of dried onions

1. Roll out the puff pastry to normal thickness as if you were making a pie.

2. Sprinkle with some of the Cheddar, onions and chives and carefully fold in half.

3. Sprinkle again with Cheddar, onions and chives and fold again. If possible, do this once more.

4. Carefully roll out the pastry again to normal thickness as if making a pie. If any of the filling falls out, just place it back in the pastry again.

5. Once rolled, cut into thin strips. You can give these a little twist before placing onto a lined baking tray.

6. Set the temperature to 200°C and bake in the oven for 15 minutes, until golden. Leave on the tray for 5 minutes before transferring to your cooling rack.

Variations:
- *Bacon and Cheese Straws* Add finely chopped bacon or pancetta for extra flavour.
- *Marmite Straws* Spread each fold with yeast extract for lovers of Marmite.
- *Stilton Straws* Use Stilton instead of Cheddar for an extra cheesy zing.
- *Chilli Straws* Add a sprinkle of paprika and chilli powder to each layer. For added kick, sprinkle with a few finely chopped chillies.
- *Garlic Butter Straws* Mix some butter, crushed garlic and mixed herbs together. Spread thinly over each layer.
- *Chocolate Straws* For chocolate lovers, try spreading each fold with chocolate spread, or sprinkles of dark chocolate chips.

● *Cinnamon Straws* Fill the folds with a generous sprinkling of cinnamon and mixed fruit (sultanas or raisins).

Or why not create some of your own?

Mini Christmas Cupcakes

Makes approximately
10–15 mini cakes

These are tiny cupcakes made in the small muffin cases – again, you can use silicon cases, available from cook shops. You can line these with a paper case if you prefer as it makes it easier to remove and serve the cupcakes. If you are on a wheat or gluten free diet, swap the flour for Doves Farm gluten and wheat-free self-raising flour.

Ingredients:
100g butter
100g sugar
2 eggs
25g cocoa, sifted
80g self-raising flour, sifted
2–3 tbsp icing sugar
Water
Coloured icing or fondant (red and green)

1. Beat the butter and sugar together until light and fluffy.

2. Add the eggs and beat well.

3. Add the sifted cocoa and flour. Fold in until thoroughly combined.

4. Place in mini silicon cases and place these on a baking tray.

5. Place on the low rack, set the temperature to 200°C and cook for 8–12 minutes. The cakes should be firm and spring back when touched.

6. Place on a cooling rack to cool.

7. Mix the icing sugar with a little water, a bit at a time, until you have a nice thick but slightly fluid icing.

8. Once the cakes are cool, place a little icing on each cake. Place red and green icing to form holly leaves and berries or if you are creative, make the leaves and berries out of green and red fondant icing.

9. Leave to set.

155

Ingredients:

200g self-raising flour

1 tsp mustard powder

Pinch of cayenne pepper

30g butter

60g mature Cheddar,
   grated

125ml milk

Cheese Scones

Why serve these delicious scones with just butter? I prefer to fill them with freshly-cooked bacon, grated cheese and salad – delicious! If you are on a wheat or gluten free diet, swap the flour for Doves Farm gluten and wheat-free self-raising and add an extra 20ml of milk to the mixture.

1. Preheat your halogen oven using the preheat setting, or set the temperature to 210°C.

2. Sift the flour into a bowl. Add the cayenne, mustard and season to taste.

3. Add the butter and rub until the mixture resembles breadcrumbs. Add the grated cheese and combine well.

4. Gradually add the milk to form a firm, but not wet, dough.

5. Place this on a floured board, and press out until 3–4cm thick. Cut with a pastry cutter and place on your greased baking tray. Brush with milk.

6. Place in the halogen oven for 10 minutes.

7. Place on a cooling rack, or serve warm!

Variations

There is no reason why you can't add finely chopped onion or, for non-vegetarians, try some some chopped cooked bacon or pancetta for a delicious savoury scone. Experiment by adding your favourite herbs. You can also use this recipe to form a cobbler topping on savoury dishes.

Iced Vanilla Cupcakes

Makes

8–15 (depending on size of cases)

Ingredients:
175g butter
175g sugar
3 eggs, beaten
175g self-raising flour
2 tsp vanilla extract or paste
3–4 tbsp icing sugar

I love these cupcakes, they look so sweet and perfect for a teatime treat. If you are on a wheat- or gluten-free diet, swap the flour for Doves Farm gluten- and wheat-free self-raising and add 30ml of water to the mixture.

1. Preheat the halogen oven using the preheat setting, or set to 200°C.

2. Cream the butter and sugar together until pale and fluffy.

3. Add the eggs a little at a time and continue to beat well.

4. Sift the flour and fold into the mixture gently.

5. When thoroughly mixed, add the vanilla extract and combine.

6. I have not been able to find a round muffin tray so I use silicon muffin cases and place these on the baking trays that come with the halogen oven accessory packs. You can comfortably fit 10 on the tray. This mixture should make 8–15 cakes depending on their size.

7. Place the mixture in the cupcake cases (for ease, I line the silicon cases with a paper case as this makes it easier to remove and serve them).

8. Place on the low rack and cook for 14–18 minutes. The cakes should be firm and spring back when touched.

9. Place on a cooling rack to cool.

10. Mix the icing sugar with a little water – add a little at a time until you have a thick but fluid icing.

11. Once the cakes are cool, place a little icing on each cake and smooth. Finish with a pastel coloured Smartie or heart-shaped sweet.

Vanilla and Chocolate Chip Smartie Cakes

Makes

8–15 (depending on size of cases)

Ingredients:

175g butter

175g sugar

3 eggs, beaten

175g self-raising flour

1 tsp vanilla essence

50g chocolate chips (can be dark, milk, white or combination)

4 tbsp icing sugar

Smarties

These are so popular with kids – the combination of vanilla, chocolate icing and Smarties is too hard to resist, even for big kids! If you are on a wheat- or gluten-free diet, swap the flour for Doves Farm gluten- and wheat-free self-raising and add 30ml of water to the mixture.

1. Preheat the halogen oven using the preheat setting or set to 200°C.

2. Cream the butter and sugar together until pale and fluffy.

3. Add the eggs a little at a time and continue to beat well.

4. Sift the flour and fold into the mixture gently.

5. When thoroughly mixed, add the vanillia essence, chocolate chips and combine.

6. I use silicon muffin cases and place these on the baking trays that come with the halogen oven accessory packs. You can comfortably fit 10 on the tray. This mixture should make 8–15 cakes depending on their size. For ease, line the silicon cases with the paper cake cases – this makes it easier when you want to remove the cases ready to serve.

7. Place on the low rack and cook for 12–18 minutes. The cakes should be firm and spring back when touched.

8. Place on a cooling rack to cool.

9. Whilst they are cooling, mix the icing sugar with a little water, a little at a time until you form a thick but fluid icing.

10. Once cool, spread the icing over the top of each cake. Finish with some Smarties.

Upside Down Blackberry and Apple Cake

Use a springform, loose-bottomed cake tin for this. It looks really impressive when turned out onto a nice cake plate or stand and sprinkled with sieved icing sugar. It's also delicious hot or cold. If you are on a wheat- or gluten-free diet, swap the flour for Doves Farm gluten- and wheat-free self-raising flour.

1. Preheat your halogen oven using the preheat setting, or set the temperature to 190°C.

2. Generously grease your cake tin with butter.

3. Place the apple slices, blackberries and 1 tablespoon of sugar in the base of your cake tin.

4. Beat the butter and sugar until light and fluffy. Add the eggs a little at a time, and then add the sifted flour. Once mixed, add the vanilla extract. Combine well.

5. Place the cake mixture over the apple and blackberries. I use a silicon spatula as it clears the bowl and is easy to use. Smooth the surface gently but don't over fuss as you don't want to lift the fruit from the bottom.

6. Place on the low rack and cook for 25–30 minutes, until the cake is cooked, firm and springs back to shape when touched.

7. When ready to serve, place an upturned plate, slightly larger than the cake top, on the top of the cake tin. Flip over so the cake tin is upside down on top of the plate, and allow the cake to drop down onto the plate. If using a springform cake tin, undo the spring, releasing the cake.

8. Sprinkle with sifted icing sugar to decorate before serving hot or cold with a spoonful of cream or crème fraîche.

Ingredients:

2–3 cooking apples, sliced
150g blackberries
1 tbsp sugar
175g butter
175g sugar
3 eggs
175g sifted self-raising
    flour
1 tsp vanilla extract

Lemon and Poppy Seed Muffins

Ingredients:

350g plain flour
1 tbsp baking powder
115g sugar
2 tbsp poppy seeds
55g butter
1 large egg
225ml milk
1 tsp lemon essence
Zest and juice of 1 lemon

If you are on a wheat- or gluten-free diet, swap the flour for Doves Farm gluten- and wheat-freeself-raising and add 30ml of water to the mixture.

1. Sift the flour and baking powder into a bowl. Stir in the sugar and poppy seeds.

2. Melt the butter. While the butter is melting, mix the egg, milk, lemon essence, juice and zest together. Add the melted butter and combine before adding this to the flour mixture.

3. Combine well.

4. When thoroughly mixed, place in your cases.

5. I use silicon muffin cases and place these on the baking trays that come with the halogen oven accessory packs. You can comfortably fit 10 on the tray. This mixture should make 6–12 cakes depending on their size. For ease, line the silicon cases with the paper cake cases – this makes it easier when you want to remove the cases ready to serve.

6. Set the temperature to 200°C and place on the low rack and cook for 12–18 minutes. The cakes should be firm and spring back when touched.

7. Place on a cooling rack to cool.

Shortcake

Makes

6–8

I used to make shortcake as a child. Don't overcook shortcake or you will end up with a hard biscuit/cake – it needs to be soft and crumbly. Serve this with whipped cream and fresh strawberries for a yummy treat, or for a less calorific choice, dunk in a cup of tea!

Ingredients:

110g self-raising flour
30g caster sugar
30g butter
75ml milk

1. Add the sifted flour into a bowl with the sugar. Combine well before rubbing in the butter until it looks like breadcrumbs (just like making pastry!).

2. Add a little milk at a time until you have a soft but not wet dough.

3. On a floured surface roll out until it is about 4–5mm thick. You can either make this one whole round of shortcake, marking out the slices and decorating them with a fork, or you can cut the dough with biscuit cutters creating lots of little biscuits.

4. Preheat your halogen oven using the preheat setting, or set the temperature to 210°C.

5. Place the shortcake on the greased browning tray. Cook for 10–12 minutes until golden.

6. Turn onto a cooling rack before serving. Once cool, store in an airtight container until needed.

Ingredients:

For the biscuits
200g butter
50g icing sugar
½ tsp vanilla paste
150g plain flour
50g cornflour

For the filling
100g butter
200g icing sugar
½ tsp vanilla extract
50g dark chocolate

Viennese Biscuits

When I was a teenager, my mum and I used to catch a bus to Exeter to go shopping for clothes and generally spend a girlie day together. We would always buy a pack of M&S Viennese Whirls and devour the whole pack on the journey home. Not much has changed since then; I can still demolish a whole portion of these delicious biscuits! This is a recipe where you really do need to use good quality butter, as margarine does not really give the same taste or result. Again, with biscuits remember they will be slightly soft when cooked and will harden once cooled.

1. Preheat your halogen oven using the preheat setting, or set the temperature to 200°C.

2. Beat the butter, icing sugar and vanilla paste together until light and fluffy.

3. Gradually add the sifted flour and cornflour until you have a firm but squeezable paste.

3. Pop this into your piping bag to create lovely swirly or straight biscuits, or if you don't want to mess around with piping bags, you can carefully spoon dollops onto a greased baking tray, making sure this fits well in your halogen oven. You will probably have enough mixture to do two batches of biscuits.

5. Place on the low rack. (If you have a height extension ring, you could bake both batches at the same time but watch the top layer as these will cook faster than the bottom layer!)

6. Bake for 10–15 minutes until golden.

7. Place on a cooling rack.

8. Whilst they are cooling, mix the butter and icing sugar together with the vanilla extract.

9. Once the biscuits are cool, use the butter icing to sandwich pairs of biscuits together. Melt the dark chocolate (either in a microwave or in bain-marie). Dip each end of the biscuits into the dark chocolate. Place on a cooling rack until chocolate is set.

10. Store in an airtight container once cooled.

Chocolate Chip Muffins

Makes

6–15 (depending on size of cases)

If you are on a wheat- or gluten-free diet, swap the flour for Doves Farm gluten and wheat free self-raising and add 30ml of water to the mixture.

1. Preheat the halogen oven using the preheat setting, or set to 200°C.

2. Mix the cocoa with the hot water and leave to one side.

3. Cream the butter and sugar together until pale and fluffy.

4. Add the eggs a little at a time and continue to beat well.

5. Sift the flour and fold into the mixture gently.

6. When thoroughly mixed, add the cocoa mixture and chocolate chips and combine.

7. I use silicon muffin cases and place these on the baking trays that come with the halogen oven accessory packs. You can comfortably fit 10 on the tray. This mixture should make 8–15 cakes depending on their size. For ease, line the silicon cases with the paper cake cases – this makes it easier when you want to remove the cases ready to serve.

8. Place on the low rack and cook for 12–18 minutes. The cakes should be firm and spring back when touched.

9. Place on a cooling rack to cool.

Ingredients:

50g cocoa

15ml boiling water

175g butter

175g sugar

3 eggs, beaten

175g self-raising flour

50g plain chocolate chips

Gingerbread Men

Ingredients:

90g butter

60g dark brown sugar

1 egg

60g black treacle

200g plain flour

½ tp bicarbonate of soda

1–2 tsp ground ginger, depending on taste

1 tsp ground cinnamon

Fresh grated nutmeg to taste

These are ideal for children to decorate and are also perfect for Christmas decorations as they last quite a long time. This is a very simple recipe which makes about 12 gingerbread men, depending on their size. Simply double up the recipe if you want to make more.

1. Cream the butter and sugar together until light and fluffy. Add the egg and the treacle and combine well.

2. Once combined, add the sifted flour, bicarbonate of soda and spices and mix until it forms a pliable but soft dough.

3. You can leave the dough in the fridge to settle for at least 30 minutes, but it can be left as long as a day if you prefer.

4. Roll the dough out on a floured surface until it reaches about 4–5mm thickness, then cut into your chosen shapes using your biscuit cutters.

5. Preheat your halogen oven using your preheat setting, or set the temperature to 180°C.

6. Place the biscuits onto a greased browning tray. Place on the low rack and cook for 10–15 minutes until they are golden. Leave to cool on the tray for 5 minutes before transferring to a cooling rack.

7. Decorate once cool. Store in an airtight container.

Delicious Iced Lemon Cakes

Makes

6–12 (depending on cupcake size)

Ingredients:

115g self-raising flour, sifted

½ tsp baking powder, sifted

115g butter

115g sugar

2 eggs

2 tbsp milk

Zest of 1 lemon

1 tsp lemon essence

4 tbsp icing sugar

Juice of lemon

If you are on a wheat- or gluten-free diet, swap the flour for Doves Farm gluten and wheat free self-raising and add 30ml of water to the mixture. Remember to only use gluten free baking powder.

1. Place all the ingredients, apart from the icing sugar and lemon juice in a bowl and mix with an electric mixer until well beaten.

2. When thoroughly mixed, place in your cases.

3. I use silicon muffin cases and place these on the baking trays that come with the halogen oven accessory packs. You can comfortably fit 10 on the tray. This mixture should make 8–15 cakes depending on their size. For ease, line the silicon cases with the paper cake cases – this makes it easier when you want to remove the cases ready to serve.

4. Place on the low rack and cook for 12–18 minutes. The cakes should be firm and spring back when touched.

5. Place on a cooling rack to cool.

6. While the cakes are cooling, mix the icing sugar with a little of the lemon juice at a time until you form a thick but fluid icing.

7. Once cooled, place the icing over the cakes. You could add some lemon zest or crystallised lemon pieces for decoration.

Ingredients:

For the cake
200ml boiling water
75g cocoa
½ tsp bicarbonate of soda
300g golden sugar
4 eggs
1 tsp vanilla paste
180ml light olive oil
200g self-raising flour

For the icing
200g dark chocolate (70% cocoa), broken into pieces
40g unsalted butter
100ml milk
50g cocoa
1 tsp vanilla essence
2 tbsp honey
Easter egg decorations (optional)

Easter Chocolate Cake

This is my son's favourite cake. I used to make it in my normal oven, but I have since swapped to the halogen oven and it works well. This is a very rich chocolate cake with a thick, rich, fudge-like icing. Decorate with mini Easter eggs or leave unadorned when making the rest of the year! If you are on a wheat- or gluten-free diet, swap the flour for Doves Farm gluten- and wheat-free self-raising and add 30ml of water to the mixture.

1. Mix your cocoa and bicarbonate of soda with the boiling water and leave to one side.

2. Grease and/or line two sponge tins

3. Meanwhile, beat the sugar and eggs together until light and creamy. Add the vanilla paste and olive oil and continue beating well.

4. Add the flour, followed by the cocoa solution. You can continue to beat the mixture at this point – for this recipe you don't need to take time over folding in your flour. This will form a batter the consistency of double cream.

5. Pour the batter into the two sponge tins.

6. Turn the halogen oven on to 170°C, with fan on full (if applicable).

7. If you have a height extension ring, you could cook the sponges together; however, if you don't have this I would advise cooking them on the low rack one at a time. If you use a height extension ring, place one sponge on the low rack and one on the high rack, but keep an eye on the top one as you may want to swap them over halfway through cooking or the top may cook a few minutes before the lower one.

8. Bake for 20–30 minutes until firm to touch and cake has pulled away slightly from the edges of the tin.

9. Once cool, place on a cooling rack while you make the icing.

10. In a bain-marie (or a bowl placed over a saucepan), add all the icing ingredients and allow to melt and blend together to form a chocolate sauce. Stir well.

11. Place one sponge, flat side up, on your serving plate or cake stand. Spread half the icing mix onto the sponge and place the remaining sponge over the top to form a sandwich.

12. Use the remaining icing to cover the top of the sponge. It will set, so don't worry if it drips down the sides of the cake. Enjoy!

Chapter 8
Bread

It is really easy to make bread in your halogen oven. If you are nervous, try some bread rolls first (all bread recipes can be used to make rolls – just cook them for less time). Remember, as the bread rises it may get closer to the element and darken too quickly. To avoid this, use a height extension ring.

Honey and Pumpkin Bread

Ingredients:

300ml warm milk

475g strong white bread
  flour

30g butter

Pinch of salt

2 tsp runny honey

7g dried yeast

75g pumpkin seeds

1. Place the flour in a bowl. Add the salt and rub in the butter. Add the honey, dried yeast and two thirds of the seeds and combine well.

2. I normally proceed next on a worktop, but you can work in a bowl if you find it easier. I place the flour on the worktop and make a large well in the centre. I pour the warm milk into the centre – a little at a time, as you may not need to use it all – then gradually stir in the edges of the flour until it is all mixed in to form a dough. If the dough is too dry, add a little more liquid; if it's too wet, add a little more flour. Bread making is all about touch and feel so enjoy the freedom.

3. On the floured surface, knead the dough. For those who have never kneaded before, you fold over the outer edge of your dough, back into the middle, and press down with your knuckles. Twist the dough around and repeat this process, continuing to press down and twist as you go, locking in air and stretching the dough for about 10 minutes (a great workout!)

4. Place the dough back in your bowl and cover with clingfilm. Set in a warm, draught free area and leave until it has doubled its size.

5. Tip the dough out again on to the floured surface and knead it again. You will notice that the dough is lighter and may fall back when you start to knead. Don't worry, it will rise again.

6. Knead for another 5 minutes, and when you're happy that it is smooth and elastic, place it in your greased loaf tin. Or, if you are making a round, freeform shape, place this on a baking tray. Sprinkle with the remaining seeds.

7. Leave again in a warm place for another 15 minutes until it starts to rise.

8. Towards the end of the 15 minutes rising time, preheat your halogen oven using the preheat setting, or set the temperature to 200°C.

9. Brush the bread with a little warm milk. If you would like the split loaf effect, you can use a sharp knife to score lengthways down the top of the loaf. When cooking, this will spread to form the split.

10. Place the bread on the low rack and cook for approximately 20–25 minutes until it has risen, is firm, and if you tap the bottom of the bread it makes a hollow sound like a drum. If the top of the bread starts to become too dark, you can add a height extension ring, which will effectively lift the element away from the top of the loaf. If you are making bread rolls using this recipe, they will take 12–15 minutes to cook.

11. Place on a cooling rack and resist the temptation to eat before it has cooled.

Multi-Seed Bread

Ingredients:

300ml warm milk or water

1 dsp malt extract

1 tsp poppy seeds

2–3 tbsp sesame seeds

2–3 tbsp sunflower seeds

3 tbsp golden linseeds

475g strong granary or
malted flour

30g butter

Pinch of salt

2 tsp molasses (or you
could use sugar or runny
honey if you prefer)

7g dried yeast

This is one of our favourites. It is actually quite hard to stick to a recipe as we normally chuck any seeds, flax and malt in willy nilly, but here is the basic format which I hope you will enjoy.

1. In a jug, mix the warm milk and the malt extract together.

2. Place the seeds and flour in a bowl. Add the salt and rub in the butter. Add the molasses and dried yeast and combine well.

3. I normally proceed next on a worktop, but you can work in a bowl if you find it easier. I place the flour on the worktop and make a large well in the centre. I pour the warm milk into the centre – a little at a time, as you may not need to use it all – then gradually stir in the edges of the flour until it is all mixed in to form a dough. If the dough is too dry, add a little more liquid; if it's too wet, add a little more flour. Bread making is all about touch and feel so enjoy the freedom.

4. On the floured surface, knead the dough. For those who have never kneaded before, you fold over the outer edge of your dough, back into the middle, and press down with your knuckles. Twist the dough around and repeat this process, continuing to press down and twist as you go, locking in air and stretching the dough for about 10 minutes (a great workout!)

5. Place the dough back in your bowl and cover with clingfilm. Set in a warm, draught free area and leave until it has doubled its size.

6. Tip the dough out again on to the floured surface and knead it again. You will notice that the dough is lighter and may fall back when you start to knead. Don't worry, it will rise again.

7. Knead for another 5 minutes, and when you're happy that it is

smooth and elastic, place it in your greased loaf tin. Or if you are making a round, freeform or crown shape (as pictured), place this on a baking tray.

8. Leave again in a warm place for another 15 minutes until it starts to rise.

9. Towards the end of the 15 minutes rising time, preheat your halogen oven using the preheat setting, or set the temperature to 200°C.

10. Brush the bread with a little warm milk and sprinkle with more seeds if you like a crunchy seeded top.

11. Place the bread on the low rack and cook for approximately 20 minutes until it has risen, is firm, and if you tap the bottom of the bread it makes a hollow sound like a drum. If you are making bread rolls using this recipe, they will take 12–15 minutes to cook.
Place on a cooling rack and resist the temptation to eat before it has cooled.

Onion and Herb Bread

200ml warm milk

50ml olive oil

475g strong white flour

30g butter

1 large onion, finely
   chopped

Small handful of freshly
   chopped herbs such as
   chives, oregano, thyme

1 tsp salt

1 tsp sugar

7g dried yeast

1. In a jug, mix the warm milk and olive oil together.

2. Place the onion, herbs and flour in a bowl. Add the salt and rub in the butter. Add the sugar and dried yeast and combine well.

3. I normally proceed next on a worktop, but you can work in a bowl if you find it easier. I place the flour on the worktop and make a large well in the centre. I pour the warm milk into the centre – a little at a time, as you may not need to use it all – then gradually stir in the edges of the flour until it is all mixed in to form a dough. If the dough is too dry, add a little more liquid; if it's too wet, add a little more flour. Bread making is all about touch and feel so enjoy the freedom.

4. On the floured surface, knead the dough. For those who have never kneaded before, you fold over the outer edge of your dough, back into the middle, and press down with your knuckles. Twist the dough around and repeat this process, continuing to press down and twist as you go, locking in air and stretching the dough for about 10 minutes (a great workout!).

5. Place the dough back in your bowl and cover with clingfilm. Set in a warm, draught free area and leave until it has doubled its size.

6. Tip the dough out again on to the floured surface and knead it again. You will notice that the dough is lighter and may fall back when you start to knead. Don't worry, it will rise again.

7. Knead for another 5 minutes, and when you're happy that it is smooth and elastic, place in your greased loaf tin. Or, if you are making a round, freeform shape, place this on a baking tray.

8. Leave again in a warm place for another 15 minutes until it starts to rise.

9. Towards the end of the 15 minutes rising time, preheat your halogen oven using the preheat setting, or set the temperature to 200°C.

9. Brush the bread with a little warm milk.
Place the bread on the low rack and cook for approximately 20 minutes until it has risen, is firm, and if you tap the bottom of the bread it makes a hollow sound like a drum. If you are making bread rolls using this recipe, they will take 12–15 minutes to cook.

10. Place on a cooling rack and resist the temptation to eat before it has cooled.

Variations
● Cheese, Onion and Chive Bread – Add 50-75g mature cheese (grated), and a small handful of freshly chopped chives in step 2, in place of the onion and herbs.
● Date and Walnut Bread – Use 200ml warm milk, and add 1 tbsp malt extract in place of the olive oil in step 1. At step 2, use 350g white flour, and add 75g walnuts (roughly chopped), 75g chopped dates, and the zest of an orange, in place of the onion and herbs. If you want to add a sticky glaze, dissolve 30g sugar in a little hot water and brush over the bread at step 10.

Brown Wholemeal Bread

Ingredients:

300ml warm milk

475g strong wholemeal
    brown flour

30g butter

Pinch of salt

7g dried yeast

1. Place the flour in a bowl. Add the salt and rub in the butter. Add the dried yeast and combine well.

2. I normally proceed next on a worktop, but you can work in a bowl if you find it easier. I place the flour on the worktop and make a large well in the centre. I pour the warm milk into the centre – a little at a time, as you may not need to use it all – then gradually stir in the edges of the flour until it is all mixed in to form a dough. If the dough is too dry, add a little more liquid; if it's too wet, add a little more flour. Bread making is all about touch and feel so enjoy the freedom.

3. On the floured surface, knead the dough. For those who have never kneaded before, you fold over the outer edge of your dough, back into the middle, and press down with your knuckles. Twist the dough around and repeat this process, continuing to press down and twist as you go, locking in air and stretching the dough for about 10 minutes (a great workout!).

4. Place the dough back in your bowl and cover with clingfilm. Set in a warm, draught free area and leave until it has doubled its size.

5. Tip the dough out again on to the floured surface and knead it again. You will notice that the dough is lighter and may fall back when you start to knead. Don't worry, it will rise again.

6. Knead for another 5 minutes, and when you're happy that it is smooth and elastic, place it in your greased loaf tin. Or, if you are making a round, freeform shape, place this on a baking tray.

7. Leave again in a warm place for another 15 minutes until it starts to rise.

8. Towards the end of the 15 minutes rising time, preheat your halogen oven using the preheat setting, or set the temperature to 200°C.

9. Brush the bread with a little warm milk.

10. Place the bread on the low rack and cook for approximately 20–25 minutes until it has risen, is firm, and if you tap the bottom of the bread it makes a hollow sound like a drum. If the top of the bread starts to become too dark, you can add a height extension ring, which will effectively lift the element away from the top of the loaf. If you are making bread rolls using this recipe, they will take 12–15 minutes to cook.

11. Place on a cooling rack and resist the temptation to eat before it has cooled.

Devonshire Split Buns

Makes

8–10

Ingredients:

250g plain white flour

250g strong white bread
  flour

7g dried yeast

2–3 tbsp caster sugar
  (depends on how sweet
  you like the dough)

60g butter, melted

300ml warm milk

Whipped or clotted cream

Jam

Icing sugar

I can't resist adding this recipe, not just because I am from
Devon but also because it brings back great memories, as these
used to be a favourite of mine when I was a child.

1. Place the flour in a bowl. Add the sugar and dried yeast and
combine well.

2. Mix the warm milk with the melted butter and combine well.

3. I normally proceed next on a worktop, but you can work in a
bowl if you find it easier. I place the flour on the worktop and
make a large well in the centre. I pour the warm milk/butter
mixture into the centre – a little at a time, as you may not need to
use it all – then gradually stir in the edges of the flour until it is all
mixed in to form a dough. If the dough is too dry, add a little
more liquid; if it's too wet, add a little more flour. Bread making is
all about touch and feel so enjoy the freedom.

4. On the floured surface, knead the dough. For those who have
never kneaded before, you fold over the outer edge of your
dough, back into the middle, and press down with your knuckles.
Twist the dough around and repeat this process, continuing to
press down and twist as you go, locking in air and stretching the
dough for about 10 minutes (a great workout!).

5. Place the dough back in your bowl and cover with clingfilm. Set
in a warm, draught free area and leave until it has doubled its size.

6. Tip the dough out again back on to the floured surface and
knead it again. You will notice that the dough is lighter and may
fall back when you start to knead. Don't worry, it will rise again.

7. Knead for another 5 minutes, and when you're happy that it is
smooth and elastic, form dough balls and place them on your
greased and floured baking tray.

8. Leave again in a warm place for another 15 minutes until it starts to rise.

9. Towards the end of the 15 minutes rising time, preheat your halogen oven using the preheat setting, or set the temperature to 200°C.

10. Brush the buns with a little warm milk.

11. Place the buns on the low rack and cook for approximately 15–20 minutes until the buns have risen, are firm, and if you tap the bottoms they make a hollow sound like a drum. If the tops of them start to become too dark, you can add a height extension ring, which will effectively lift the element away from the top of the buns.

12. Place on a cooling rack.

13. Once cooled split open with a sharp knife and fill with jam and whipped or clotted cream. Sprinkle with a little icing sugar before serving. Delicious!

Chelsea Buns

Ingredients:

For the bread

225g strong white bread
   flour

2 tsp sugar

7g dried yeast

30g butter

1 large egg, beaten

125ml warm milk

For the filling

30g butter

50–75g dried fruit

40g brown sugar

2 tsp cinnamon

Sprinkle of sugar to
   decorate

1. In a large bowl, add the flour, sugar and dried yeast. Combine well.

2. Rub in the butter to form a texture similar to breadcrumbs. Once combined, add the egg and warm milk. Combine well to form a dough.

3. On a floured surface, knead the dough for 5 minutes. Place the dough back in the bowl, cover and keep in a warm place for 30–40 minutes or until it has doubled in size.

4. Preheat your halogen oven using the preheat setting, or set the temperature to 180°C.

5. When the dough is ready, place back on the floured surface and knead again for another 5 minutes.

6. Roll into a large rectangle, roughly 30cm, making sure there are no breaks in the dough.

7. Melt the remaining butter either with the heat of the halogen oven or in a saucepan (though make sure it does not burn).

8. Leaving a gap of approximately 2cm around the edge, cover the remaining dough with a brush of melted butter. Finish by evenly distributing your dried fruit, brown sugar and cinnamon.

9. Holding the end of the dough nearest to you, gently lift and roll to create one large sausage.

10. Using a sharp serrated knife, slice it into 2cm slices. Place these on a well-greased or lined baking tray. You can place them so they could touch when risen – allowing you to pull them apart when cooked.

11. Place in the halogen oven on the low rack. (You may need to do this in batches or use a height extension ring to enable you to use two racks – though cooking times will vary as the top rack will cook quicker than the bottom rack.)

12. Cook for 20–25 minutes until golden and risen. Remove and place on a cooling rack.

13. Sprinkle with sugar before serving hot or cold.

Index